FAMILYLIFE
HOMEBUILDERS
COUPLES SERIES

BUILDING YOUR MATE'S SELF-ESTEEM

DENNIS AND BARBARA RAINEY

PERSONAL STUDY GUIDE

"UNLESS THE LORD BUILDS THE HOUSE
THEY LABOR IN VAIN WHO BUILD IT."
Psalm 127:1

Gospel Light

How to
Let the Lord
Build Your House

FamilyLife is a part of Campus Crusade for Christ International, an evangelical Christian organization founded in 1951 by Bill Bright. FamilyLife was started in 1976 to help fulfill the Great Commission by strengthening marriages and families and then equipping them to go to the world with the gospel of Jesus Christ. Our FamilyLife Marriage Conference, known as "A Weekend to Remember," is held in most major cities throughout the United States and is one of the fastest-growing marriage conferences in America today. Information on all resources offered by FamilyLife may be obtained by either writing or calling us at the address and telephone number listed below

■

The HomeBuilders Couples Series: A small-group Bible study dedicated to making your family all that God intended.

Building Your Mate's Self-Esteem—Study Guide
ISBN 0-8307-1616-5

Dennis Rainey, Director
FamilyLife
P.O. Box 23840
Little Rock, AR 72221-3840
(501) 223-8663

A Ministry of Campus Crusade for Christ International
Bill Bright, Founder and President

Published by Gospel Light, Ventura, California 93006

CONTENTS

ACKNOWLEDGMENTS

Jeff Tikson is the best utility infielder we've seen. You helped hatch this idea four years ago and played a key role in seeing this whole **HomeBuilders Couples Series** become a reality. You've coached, encouraged, asked tough questions, and helped sharpen this material immeasurably. Thanks not only for the hours you spent serving us on this project (so we could complete it), but for your enduring friendship as well. God has great things in store for you in the days ahead.

Hard work and a heart for people are synonyms for Jerry Wunder. Thanks for pushing us and this project along. You know that because of the leadership role you've played in FamilyLife, you've given us the precious commodity of time—time to write, create, sharpen, and give birth to this small-group study. It wouldn't have happened if you hadn't come to join our team when you did. Thanks, Jerry (and you too Sheryl, for covering the home base while he was gone), for the grueling trip you made with Jeff to find the best publisher for this series.

Others helped as well: Lee Burrell was a servant of servants on this project—again. No one in responsibility is effective without a great secretary—and we have had a pair of them. Sue Stinson, you are a compassionate angel in disguise—thanks for the juggling act you continually perform. Elizabeth Reha, you may not be a flying nun, but you have been a delight to our office. You are missed. A.J. Laubhan and Sam Naff are true leaders—thanks for comprising the leadership team that drives all the work we do forward. Thanks to Ted Grove and Jeff Lord for all the work on field-testing this study. Fred Hitchcock, your editing was once again on target. And to Jeff and Brenda Schulte, you two are a priceless pair who (in just six short months) have been a gift to our family.

Thanks go also to Wes Haystead for his wisdom and expertise on the **HomeBuilders** project.

If you don't know Julie Denker then you should. She's got a great grin and a tenacious spirit. If you don't think so, then just try a game of basketball or a game of slow-pitch softball with her. She has been the steady plodder of **The HomeBuilders Couples Series**. Julie, our deepest gratitude goes to you for the hundreds of hours of editing and tracking this project. It is to you that this book is dedicated.

How to
Let the Lord
Build Your House

and not labor in vain

INTRODUCTION

What Is The HomeBuilders Couples Series?

Do you remember the first time you fell in love? That junior high —or elementary school—"crush" stirred your affections with little or no effort on your part. We use the term "falling in love" to describe the phenomenon of suddenly discovering our emotions have been captured by someone delightful.

Unfortunately, our society tends to make us think that all loving relationships should be equally as effortless. Thus, millions of couples, Christians included, approach their marriage certain that the emotions they feel will carry them through any difficulties. And millions of couples quickly learn that a good marriage does not automatically happen.

Otherwise intelligent people, who would not think of buying a car, investing money, or even going to the grocery store without some initial planning, enter into marriage with no plan of how to make their marriage succeed.

But God has already provided the plan, a set of blueprints for a truly godly marriage. His plan is designed to enable two people to grow together in a mutually satisfying relationship, and then to look beyond their own marriage to others. Ignoring this plan leads only to isolation and separation between husband and wife, the pattern so evident in the majority of homes today. Even when great energy is expended, failure to follow God's blueprints results in wasted effort, bitter disappointment—and, in far too many cases, divorce.

In response to this need in marriages today, FamilyLife of Campus Crusade for Christ is developing a series of small-group Bible studies called **The HomeBuilders Couples Series.** This series is designed to answer one question for couples:

How Do You Build a Distinctively Christian Marriage?

It is our hope that in answering this question with the biblical blueprints for building a home, we will see the development of growing, thriving marriages filled with the love of Jesus Christ.

FamilyLife of Campus Crusade for Christ is committed to strengthening your family. We hope **The HomeBuilders Couples Series** will assist you and your church as it equips couples in building godly homes.

This study, **Strengthening Your Mate's Self-Esteem**, is designed to provide the basis upon which a godly marriage can be built. It is composed of eight sessions, each built around a concept that will enrich your marriage in the weeks that follow.

The Bible: Your Blueprints for a Godly Marriage

The Bible is alive, it speaks to me;
it has feet, it runs after me;
it has hands, it lays its hold on me.

Martin Luther

You will notice as you proceed through this study that the Bible is referred to frequently as the final authority on the issues of life and marriage. Although written centuries ago, this Book still speaks clearly and powerfully about the conflicts and struggles faced by men and women. The Bible is God's Word, His blueprints for building a godly home and for dealing with the practical issues of living.

While Scripture has only one primary interpretation, there may be several appropriate applications. Some of the passages used in this series were not originally written with marriage in mind, but they can be applied practically to the husband-wife relationship.

W e encourage you to have a Bible with you for each session. The *New American Standard Bible* and the *New International Version* are two excellent English translations which make the Bible easy to understand.

Ground Rules for These Sessions

T hese sessions are designed to be enjoyable and informative—and nonthreatening. Three simple ground rules will help insure that everyone feels comfortable and gets the most out of the series:

1. Share nothing about your marriage that will embarrass your mate.

2. You may pass on any question you do not want to answer.

3. Each time between sessions, complete the **HomeBuilders Project** (a few questions for each couple to discuss). Share one result at the next group meeting.

Resources

F amilyLife recommends these outstanding aids to maximize your **HomeBuilders** study experience.

1. If doing this as a couple, we would recommend one Study Guide for each spouse. The Leader's Guide would also be very beneficial.

2. If you have been to the FamilyLife Marriage Conference, you will find the **FamilyLife Marriage Conference Manual** to be a useful tool as you go through **The HomeBuilders Couples Series**.

3. Your best resource is one another—others can help us maximize our lives as we learn to be accountable for our actions and lives. Be accountable to one another and to another couple for the session and projects completion.

HOMEBUILDERS
PRINCIPLES

HomeBuilders Principle #1: It is only as you help your mate understand the right value system, God's truth as found in the Scriptures, that you can help your mate slay the phantom and proceed in becoming all God wants him or her to be.

HomeBuilders Principle #2: Everyone needs to be accepted by at least one other person—his or her mate.

HomeBuilders Principle #3: It is only as your mate experiences the security of your unconditional love that he or she will risk being real in the marriage relationship.

HomeBuilders Principle #4: It is essential that you and your mate experience and express God's forgiveness through Jesus Christ if you are to put your pasts behind you and have hope for the future.

HomeBuilders Principle #5: In dealing with your mate's past, it is far better to be kind and forgiving than condemning.

HomeBuilders Principle #6: Praise is the lubricant of relationships. It reduces friction and increases wear.

HomeBuilders Principle #7: By giving the freedom to risk failing, you will help your mate begin to separate self-worth from performance.

HomeBuilders Principle #8: When you give your mate the freedom to risk failing, failure can become a tutor and not a judge.

HomeBuilders Principle #9: Through prayer we can ask God for wisdom, which will enable us as a couple to handle the pressures of life.

HomeBuilders Principle #10: The Holy Spirit is God's personal provision for discerning His direction and bringing peace and order to your life, marriage, and family.

HomeBuilders Principle #11: Accountability between husband and wife is the anchor that God has given to us for finding security, protection, and balance in the storms of life.

HomeBuilders Principle #12: God has appointed you as the husband to build your wife's self-esteem.

HomeBuilders Principle #13: Your husband's value and security as a man is most affected by you, his wife. You are the most important person in his life.

HomeBuilders Principle #14: A couple finds a sense of eternal value and self-esteem as they get to know God and invest their lives in the cause which will outlive them.

HomeBuilders Principle #15: Jesus Christ did not go to the cross just so we could have happy marriages or a healthy self-esteem, but so that we would love Him, love one another, and go to the world with the greatest news ever announced.

A WORD ABOUT
SELF-ESTEEM

In recent days the subject of self-esteem has come under fire by some Christians. While we agree with much of the criticism of current teachings on this subject, we do not agree that this subject of self-esteem is unbiblical.

First, we believe God wants us who are Christians (those who have experienced forgiveness of sins and the new birth through faith in the Person of Jesus Christ and His finished work on the cross) to realize *who we are*—children of God.

Second, the focus of this study is not on your "self," but on *your* spouse's self-esteem. Thus, the need we are addressing in both our book, **Building Your Mate's Self-Esteem**, and in this **HomeBuilders** study is not how to manipulate your mate to build you up, but rather how to help your mate realize who he or she is as a Child of God.

Third, perhaps a good subtitle to our book and this study would be "How to Minister to Your Mate." In these pages you will find practical ways in how to build up (edify), strengthen, and encourage your mate.

It is our hope that as a couple you will benefit from this study and the accountability to others **The HomeBuilders Couples Series** provides. May you be successful in building up one another and in building your home.

About Our Book:
Building Your Mate's Self-Esteem

Thanks for choosing **The HomeBuilders Couples Series** to strengthen your marriage. **Building Your Mate's Self-Esteem** is a small-group adaptation of our book **Building Your Mate's Self-Esteem.** We surveyed over 17,000 individuals at our FamilyLife Marriage Conferences and asked them what they felt was the greatest need in their marriages. Well over 50 percent chose this topic. For the better part of two years we researched and wrote what we believe is an intensely practical book to help you in an area of need we all experience. And now after another two years of writing and field-testing, we are pleased to offer this study to build Christian marriages.

We have designed this particular study to stand alone without your having to read our book, **Building Your Mate's Self-Esteem**. And although there is plenty of material in this Bible study for any couple to process, we know that many will want to purchase our book for gaining even a better understanding of how to minister to their mate.

Because we sought to keep this study at eight sessions we had to eliminate valuable concepts that we discussed in depth in our book. Among the topics we discuss in our book (but are not in this study) are:

■ How to build up your mate when you encounter the storms of life.

■ Ten clues that your mate will give you that he needs your help in building his self-esteem.

■ How to encourage your mate to obey God.

■ How to please your mate and add sizzle to romance in your marriage.

■ How to help your mate develop good friends who will build his self-esteem.

■ And the importance of perseverance and an enduring commitment in your relationship.

■ Plus additional projects for applying these principles to your marriage.

You may want to read the book and the chapters which cover the topics you'll be discussing in your study. Or you may benefit by reading the book after you've completed this study. Whatever you decide, we're excited that you've chosen to join a rapidly growing number of Christians who are committed to building godly homes and leaving a godly legacy.

Now, let's begin . . .

Marriage provides one of life's best relationships for building another's self-esteem.

STRENGTHENING SELF-ESTEEM

LAW OF GIVING	LAW OF UNDERSTANDING	LAW OF SOWING AND REAPING	LAW OF DIVINE SUFFICIENCY

THE FOUNDATION

1. List below the names of the couples in your group, their occupations, and the number of years they have been married:

Names   Occupations   Years

_____   _____   _____

_____   _____   _____

_____   _____   _____

_____   _____   _____

_____   _____   _____

_____   _____   _____

_____   _____   _____

2. Answer *one* of these questions:

■ What was a humorous or embarrassing incident from your dating, honeymoon, or early marriage?

■ What did your mate think of you after your first date?

■ What unique experience have you and your mate had that most people in this group probably don't know about (job, place visited, hobby, sport, how you became engaged—something unusual)?

A. The Need

1. One of the greatest needs of every individual is to be built up (encouraged, strengthened) in the task of living. What are some reasons this is true?

_____

_____

2. Many marriages consist of two people, each trying to get the other to build him or her up. Why do you think this happens?

_____

_____

3. Scripture often exhorts Christians to build up one another. (The word *edify* is frequently used. It comes from two Greek words: *oikos*, which means "a home," and *dimeo*, which means "to build." Therefore, "edify" literally means "to build a home.") How do you think 1 Thessalonians 5:11 and 15 apply to a married couple?

_____

_____

4. A crucial ingredient in any successful marriage is for both people to recognize the importance of building up their mate. How do Ephesians 5:25, 29, 31 and Romans 14:19 spell this out?

_____

_____

5. Why do you think husbands and wives are often reluctant to build up their mates?

_____

_____

6. Even when we want to build up our mate, we often do not succeed because we do not understand the condition of our mate's self-esteem. In your own words, what is self-esteem?

_____

_____

7. How does self-esteem affect a person—

a. positively? _____

_____

b. negatively? _____

_____

8. What added insight about self-esteem do you gain from Romans 12:3?

_____

_____

Now that you are beginning to understand how important you are to building your mate's self-esteem, let's take a look at one of the major influences on it.

B. The Culprit—The Wrong Standards of Comparison

As we compare ourselves with "apparently successful people," perfect images from the media, and our own unreal ideals, we create an unattainable standard for ourselves. This unattainable standard is like a phantom by which we measure ourselves. When we compare the reality of our lives (our true strengths and weaknesses) with our "phantom," the result can be feelings of inferiority and insecurity.

BARBARA RAINEY'S PHANTOM	DENNIS RAINEY'S PHANTOM
The perfect wife, mother and friend, always patient and kind with an ideal house and family. She is well organized, with a perfect balance between being disciplined and flexible. Her house is always neat and well decorated, and her children obey the first time, every time.	The fully competent husband, father, leader and employer who is always on top of every situation. He rises early, has a quiet time reading the Bible and praying, and then jogs several seven-minute miles. After breakfast with his family, he presents a fifteen-minute devotional.

1. Briefly describe your personal "phantom." (Be specific)

_____

_____

2. What is the impact of your phantom on your self-esteem?

_____

_____

3. Briefly explore why this unattainable standard is a fantasy and is really unachievable for *any* human being.

_____

_____

4. What can you do to help slay your mate's phantom?

_____

_____

HomeBuilders Principle #1: It is only as you help your mate understand the right value system, God's truth as found in the Scriptures, that you can help your mate slay the phantom and proceed in becoming all God wants him or her to be.

C. God's Truth: A New Standard of Comparison

1. Select one of the following statements of God's truth about a Christian (a person who has placed faith in Christ for forgiveness of sins) and explain why that truth brings worth and value to your mate:

a. You have value because God created you (Psalm 139:13–16).

b. You are loved in that Christ died for you (Romans 5:8).

c. You are God's own child (John 1:12).

d. You have been given a high purpose for your life (Ephesians 2:10).

_____

_____

2. Discuss why it is that these truths are difficult to grasp on a daily basis.

_____

_____

_____

D. Laws That Liberate

As we begin building up our mate's self-esteem, there are some fundamental principles from Scripture which apply to this lifelong process. A good grasp of the following four "laws" will enable you to minister wisely to your mate.

1. **The Law of Giving**—"Give, and it will be given to you; good measure, pressed down, shaken together, running over, they will pour into your lap. For whatever measure you deal out to others, it will be dealt to you in return" (Luke 6:38).

a. Identify how the Law of Giving affects one's self-esteem and overflows to another's self-esteem.

_____

_____

_____

b. How would you apply this first law to your marriage?

_____

_____

_____

2. The Law of Sowing and Reaping

—"Do not be deceived, God is not mocked; for whatever a man sows, this he will also reap" (Galatians 6:7).

a. What can a person expect to harvest from sowing seeds of patience, encouragement, affirmation, and belief in another person?

_____

_____

b. What would occur from a lifetime of sowing negative seeds?

_____

_____

3. The Law of Understanding

—"By wisdom a house is built, and by understanding it is established" (Proverbs 24:3).

How does understanding your mate help you build and establish his or her self-esteem?

_____

_____

4. The Law of Divine Sufficiency

—"Not that we are adequate in ourselves to consider anything as coming from ourselves, but our adequacy is from God" (2 Corinthians 3:5).

"I can do all things through Him (Christ) who strengthens me" (Philippians 4:13).

How would these verses help a person who has a poor self-esteem?

_____

_____

Just as darkness flees the light, so your mate's phantom will flee the light of God's truth. By continually applying these laws, you will encourage your mate to be all that God intends.

"For nothing will be impossible with God." (Luke 1:37)

Close your time together by sharing one thing you hope to gain from this study.

_____

_____

(to be completed as a couple)

Complete the following sentences and share them with your mate:

1. One of the things I appreciate most about you is . . .

_____

_____

2. One of the things you do which encourages me most is . . .

_____

_____

3. Conclude your time by reading together the following personal pledge statement:

> **"I pledge to you that I will use the next six weeks of this HomeBuilders study to build, strengthen, and encourage our marriage. I will make this study a priority in my schedule by faithfully keeping our "dates," working through the projects, and participating in the group discussions. You have my word on it."**
>
> **(signed)** _____

Will you honor your mate by making this pledge *your* special commitment to him or her for the coming weeks? If so, sign your name in the space underneath this pledge in **your mate's** study guide to document your commitment.

Make a date with your mate to meet in the next few days to complete **HomeBuilders Project #1**. This will aid you in building one another's self-esteem. At the next session you will be asked to share one thing from this experience.

Date	Time	Location

■

Recommended Reading

Building Your Mate's Self-Esteem   **by Dennis and Barbara Rainey**

■ "Giving Your Mate a New Image," "Slaying the Phantom," "Detecting the Clues," and "Nine Laws That Liberate" are the subjects covered in chapters 1-4, pp. 21-69, in **Building Your Mate's Self-Esteem**. These will help you consider further the issues discussed in this session.

■ Before your next session you will want to read chapter 5, pp. 70-82, in **Building Your Mate's Self-Esteem**. This chapter deals with the issue of "Dealing with the Good, the Bad, and the Otherwise in Your Mate."

As a Couple—5-10 Minutes

Review the **CONSTRUCTION** section you shared in this session.

Individually—10-15 Minutes

Read through the list of descriptions on the next page. For each area, use the letters shown to describe yourself and your mate. Star the ones that tend to be major struggle areas. As you evaluate your mate, be careful about being harsh or "dumping" on him or her. A sensitive approach to your mate on this **first** project is a must.

U = Usually   S = Sometimes   R = Rarely

Self	DESCRIPTION	Mate
___	Fears change	___
___	Is introspective	___
___	Fears rejection	___
___	Seeks to identify with accomplishments	___
___	Is critical of self	___
___	Is easily discouraged	___
___	Is preoccupied with past	___
___	Is defensive	___
___	Is driven by performance	___
___	Talks negatively of self	___
___	Seeks identity through position	___
___	Lacks decisiveness	___
___	Is critical of others	___
___	Tends to question self	___
___	Compares self with others	___
___	Fears failure	___
___	Tends to believe the worst about a situation	___
___	Can be paralyzed by own inadequacies	___
___	Seeks identity through accumulation of wealth	___
___	Has difficulty establishing meaningful relationships	___
___	Hides weaknesses	___
___	Attempts to control others to make self look good	___
___	Is generally satisfied with self	___
___	Seeks identity through association with significant others	___
___	Is overly self-conscious	___
___	Has negative feelings about self	___
___	Has unreal expectations of self	___
___	Worries about what others think	___
___	Needs continual approval	___
___	Is insecure around others	___
___	Has difficulty opening up	___
___	Takes things personally	___

27

Interact As a Couple—30–35 Minutes

Be aware: this project can be painful but the process is worth it.

1. Compare and discuss your list with your mate's list. How well do you know where your mate struggles? Which one or two areas tend to be major struggling points for your mate? For you?

_____

_____

2. Write down what your mate recommends you do to help him or her in major problem area(s).

_____

_____

3. Read 2 Corinthians 12:9–10 and discuss how you are to view your inadequacies and weaknesses.

_____

_____

4. Close by praying for one another. Thank God for your mate. Thank Him that He wants to use you to help your mate see who he or she is in His eyes. Ask Him to use "weaknesses" as an opportunity for His power to be demonstrated in one another's lives.

Remember to bring your calendar for **MAKE A DATE** to your next session.

Focus

Help your mate experience the liberating power of unconditional love by accepting him or her completely.

STRENGTHENING SELF-ESTEEM

	ACCEPTING UNCONDITIONALLY		
LAW OF GIVING	LAW OF UNDERSTANDING	LAW OF SOWING AND REAPING	LAW OF DIVINE SUFFICIENCY

THE FOUNDATION

1. Begin this session by sharing one thing you learned from **HomeBuilders Project #1**.

2. Answer *one* of the following questions:

a. What qualities most attracted you to your mate? (Share 3–5 if possible.)

b. Share one practical insight gained from doing the Self-Esteem Inventory during the week.

_____

_____

_____

_____

_____

One of the greatest human needs we have is the need for unconditional love and acceptance. Unfortunately, many of us find that the fear of rejection can be a controlling influence in our lives and marriages.

A. The Need

1. Why do people often fear rejection?

_____

_____

2. What insight about the fear of rejection do you find in Genesis 3:1-10?

_____

_____

3. a. What are some ways that the fear of rejection can affect a marriage relationship? (Be specific.)

_____

_____

b. How do people try to protect themselves from rejection in a marriage? (Be specific.)

_____

_____

4. Many of us wear a mask over a sensitive or fragile area in our lives in order to assure acceptance. In what area of your life did you wear a mask in your dating or early marriage relationship? Have you removed it? If so, what has been the effect of removing that mask on your marriage relationship? Have you ever been tempted to put that "mask" back on? If so, why?

_____

_____

5. What do you find in Ephesians 2:4–7 that is true about your ultimate acceptance by God?

_____

_____

> **HomeBuilders Principle #2: Everyone needs to be accepted by at least one other person—his or her mate.**

B. The Process of Acceptance

The process of accepting your mate involves two crucial components:

■ Commitment to acceptance; and

■ Communication of that acceptance to the other person.

I accept you Amy, because I decided to love you regardless as I sang to you on our wedding day

1. Commitment to Acceptance

Often today, commitment has been robbed of any real and lasting meaning. The Scripture, however, speaks of commitment in concrete terms which we can all understand.

Turn to Genesis 2:21–25 to find two practical and tangible phases of acceptance of your mate as illustrated in the experience of the first couple, Adam and Eve. The commitment to acceptance involves two phases:

■ Phase One: Receiving God's Provision

■ Phase Two: Constructing a Relationship

a. Phase One: Receiving God's Provision (Genesis 2:23)

The first phase of acceptance is seen in verse 23 when Adam receives Eve as God's perfect provision for his needs.

(1) Why do you think Adam could receive a woman he didn't know? Whom in this passage did Adam know?

_____

_____

_____

(2) How do we know that Adam totally accepted Eve?

_____

_____

(3) With this in mind, how should you accept your mate and how should you communicate this acceptance *to* your mate?

_____

_____

_____

33

We have all heard of the cliche, "opposites attract." Yet the same differences which attracted you to your mate often become a source of aggravation and even rejection after we marry.

(4) How are you and your mate different?

_____

_____

(5) How have you seen God use these differences in your lives?

_____

_____

b. Phase Two: Constructing a Relationship

In Genesis 2:25, the man and woman were both naked (without masks, covering, or disguise) "and they were not ashamed" (had no fear of rejection). In other words, they were building a relationship marked by transparency and openness. We find the basis of this trusting acceptance in verse 24.

(1) What are the three components of acceptance shown in verse 24?

_____

_____

_____

(2) How does each of these three components demonstrate a commitment to acceptance?

_____

_____

2. Communication of Acceptance

As you have probably already discovered, what communicates love and acceptance to you doesn't always communicate the same message to your mate. You must adapt your message and method of communicating to the unique needs of your mate.

a. How has your mate accepted you by demonstrating at least one of these descriptions of perfect love (1 Corinthians 13)?

Love . . .
—is patient   _____

—is kind   _____

—is never jealous   _____

—is never arrogant   _____

—is never provoked   _____

—is never boastful   _____

—seeks your best good   _____

—is never failing   _____

b. Why did this "demonstration" make you feel accepted? What effect did it have on your self-esteem?

_____

_____

Just as 1 Corinthians 13 describes perfect love, 1 John 4:18 describes its effect:

> "There is no fear in love;
> but perfect love casts out fear . . ."

c. In what way does perfect love, this unconditional acceptance, cast out the fear of rejection?

_____

_____

d. What would you recommend to a person who has difficulty communicating unconditional love and acceptance to his mate?

_____

_____

e. Think of a time when you have experienced love and acceptance from your mate. What positive effect did that have on your self-esteem?

_____

_____

HomeBuilders Principle #3: It is only as your mate experiences the security of your unconditional love that he or she will risk being real in the marriage relationship.

---

f. What insights have you gained which support **HomeBuilders Principle #3**?

_____

_____

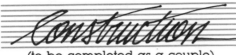

(to be completed as a couple)

1. In your marriage relationship, what brings *you* the greatest sense of acceptance, well-being, and security?

_____

_____

2. What do you think brings *your mate* the greatest sense of acceptance, well-being, and security?

_____

_____

3. Now share your answers and discuss how you can better communicate acceptance to your mate.

4. Pray together for God's help in accepting one another.

To Further Strengthen Your Marriage

Over 130,000 individuals have experienced "A Weekend To Remember" at our FamilyLife Marriage Conferences. If you'd like a free brochure giving details of this marriage enrichment weekend at quality hotels in nearly 50 cities throughout the U.S., then write:

FamilyLife Marriage Conferences
P.O. Box 23840
Little Rock, AR 72221-3840

Make a date with your mate to meet in the next few days to complete **HomeBuilders Project #2**. This will aid you as a couple in building one another's self-esteem. Your leader will ask you at the next session to share one thing from this experience.

Date	Time	Location

■

Building Your Mate's Self-Esteem

Building Your Mate's Self-Esteem   by Dennis and Barbara Rainey

■ "Giving Your Mate a New Image," "Slaying the Phantom," "Detecting the Clues," "Nine Laws That Liberate," and "Dealing with the Good, the Bad and the Otherwise in Your Mate" are the subjects covered in chapters 1-5, pp. 21-81 in **Building Your Mate's Self-Esteem**. These will help you consider further the issues discussed in this session.

■ Before your next session you will want to read chapter 6, pp. 82-101. This chapter deals with the issue of "Helping Your Mate Clean Out the Attic of the Past."

■

As a Couple—5–10 Minutes

Briefly review the **CONSTRUCTION** section. Share the most meaningful insight you received.

Individually—35–40 Minutes

1. List below any areas where you do feel accepted and not afraid to be . . .

_____

_____

_____

2. List below any areas where you are afraid to be transparent, afraid of being rejected, or don't feel fully accepted by your mate.

_____

_____

_____

3. a. List areas in which your mate may be afraid to share any innermost thoughts with you out of fear of being rejected —areas you feel your mate intentionally keeps private.

_____

_____

_____

b. How have you contributed to your mate's covering up in these areas?

_____

_____

_____

4. Are there differences or weaknesses in your mate that you are grateful for? Or that continually bother you? List them and thank God for them.

_____

_____

_____

5. Do you trust your mate partially or totally? Why or why not?

_____

_____

6. How can your mate better express love so that trust between the two of you can be built and maintained? Give one or two specific ways.

_____

_____

7. How can you better express the kind of love to your mate that "casts out all fear"?

_____

_____

8. How can your mate pray positively for you? List at least three areas.

a. _____

b. _____

c. _____

9. Will you accept your mate from God as His provision for you— including both strengths and weaknesses that have a divine purpose in your life? Write out a one- or two-paragraph statement expressing love, commitment, and acceptance for your mate. Be sure to include a statement about casting out fear of rejection. Sign it and date it. (Use additional paper if needed.)

_____

_____

_____

_____

Interact As a Couple—15-20 Minutes

1. Go through your project together, sharing with each other what you wrote down and observed.

2. Read your written statements to each other.

3. Finish by praying positively for each other in the areas you noted during your individual times. Thank God that out of the five billion people in the world, there is not another more suited to be your mate than the one sitting there with you, your mate.

Remember to bring your calendar for **MAKE A DATE** to your next session.

Focus

*Build hope and perspective by helping
your mate understand how his or
her past affects his or her
self-esteem today.*

STRENGTHENING SELF-ESTEEM

	ACCEPTING UNCONDITIONALLY	**PUTTING THE PAST IN PERSPECTIVE**	
LAW OF GIVING	LAW OF UNDERSTANDING	LAW OF SOWING AND REAPING	LAW OF DIVINE SUFFICIENCY

THE FOUNDATION

1. Begin this session by sharing one thing you learned from **HomeBuilders Project #2**.

2. Choose two of the following to share:

a. Your nickname(s) from your childhood or youth

b. A positive experience that happened to you while growing up (something good someone said about you publicly, something you accomplished that continues to bring a glow, etc.)

c. An embarrassing experience from your childhood or adolescence that still makes you cringe when thinking about it (but which you really can laugh about now)

d. A significant experience in the past that has shaped your self-esteem for good or bad

_____

_____

_____

_____

A Special Message

Because no one is perfect, all of us bring to marriage some negative experiences. Without realizing it, our past mistakes and wrong choices (as well as those made by others) can have a profound impact on us today. It is not the purpose of this session to embarrass anyone, to reopen old wounds, or to create unnecessary guilt for something which God has already forgiven.

It is important, however, that two things do occur:

■ You recognize the impact the past has had on you for good and bad; and

■ you learn some biblical principles that will enable you to put the past behind you (and help your mate leave his, or her, past behind as well).

Although a Christian couple cannot duplicate the wisdom and insight of a professional counselor, you can build a relationship in which you and your mate lovingly remind each other of God's forgiveness, offering biblical counsel in putting away bitterness and guilt.

If there is something you feel you and your mate cannot work through, then we recommend you see a competent Christian counselor or your pastor.

This session may touch some sensitive areas in your past and/or your mate's past. Throughout the session and the **HomeBuilders Project**, remember to share nothing that—

■ may hurt or embarrass you, your mate, or others; or

■ you do not feel safe in sharing.

45

I feel like our marriage involves three parties—myself, my husband, and **his** past." This statement illustrates the impact of the past on the present. While we cannot change our mate's past, we can help our mate respond positively to even the most negative experiences which may have occurred.

A. The Effect of the Past on Self-Esteem

1. How does the past affect self-esteem, both positively and negatively?

_____

_____

2. Why is the past often difficult to discuss?

_____

_____

For this session we have categorized the past into three areas:

■ Parents

■ Peers (childhood siblings, friends, and acquaintances)

■ Past in general (school, career, marriage, relationships, etc.)

3. How did David feel about his past sins?

WHAT HE DID (2 Samuel 11)	HOW HE FELT (Psalm 51:3, 17)
■ Adultery ■ Deception ■ Murder	

4. How have your **parents**, and your relationship with them, affected your self-esteem—

a. positively? _____

_____

b. negatively? _____

_____

5. Growing up, how did **peers** affect your self-esteem?

_____

_____

6. How can the **past in general** affect your self-esteem? (This category can include such areas as successes or problems with spouse, school, career, loss of child, a failure in a relationship; or a major failure of some kind.)

_____

_____

7. What can happen to the self-esteem of the person who has been wronged and refuses to forgive?

_____

_____

8. Why are the exhortations of Ephesians 4:26 and 31 important for us to heed?

_____

_____

HomeBuilders Principle #4: It is essential that you and your mate experience and express God's forgiveness through Jesus Christ if you are to put your pasts behind you and have hope for the future.

B. How to Help Your Mate Put the Past in Perspective

1. What unique solution does Christianity offer which affects one's view of past mistakes? (2 Corinthians 5:17)

_____

_____

2. What if some of us may not feel like a new creature? What encouragement is offered in Isaiah 43:18–19?

_____

_____

48

3. In light of the apostle Paul's past (Acts 8:1, 3—Paul's Jewish name was Saul), how do his writings help deal with the past?

a. 2 Corinthians 5:21

(1) _____

_____

b. Romans 8:1

(2) _____

_____

c. Philippians 3:12–14

(3) _____

_____

(4) _____

_____

d. Ephesians 4:32

(5) _____

_____

(6) _____

e. Philippians 4:8–9

(7) _____

_____

(8) _____

_____

Share which principle is most meaningful to you and why.

4. We read in Ephesians 4:32 that we are to "forgive just as God in Christ has forgiven you." To forgive means to put away the right to punish another. Since God has given up His right to punish us, how should you and your mate respond to each other's past mistakes?

_____

_____

5. How can you experience God's forgiveness? (1 John 1:9)

_____

_____

The word *confess* means to "agree with."

6. Earlier we saw David's guilt. Read Psalm 51:1-4, 7, and 10. What is his response to that guilt?

_____

_____

7. What if your mate doesn't believe God has forgiven past sins, or if he or she still feels guilty after admitting failure and claiming God's forgiveness? What does this say about God and His Word?

_____

_____

8. How can you help your mate "forget what lies behind" and experience the reality of 1 John 1:9?

_____

_____

HomeBuilders Principle #5: In dealing with your mate's past, it is far better to be kind and forgiving than condemning.

---

9. What is the most important thing you learned in this session?

_____

_____

(to be completed as a couple)

While each of the areas of the past provides both positive and negative influences, it is the negative ones that cause us problems in the present. As you and your mate talk about each other's past, do not overlook the positive influences while you attempt to help each other deal with the negative situations.

1. Generally speaking, your and your mate's present self-esteem are negatively influenced by past mistakes of:

■ Parents

■ Peers

■ Past in general (self-choices/actions)

With your mate, rank the negative influence that these three areas of the past have had on your and your mate's self-esteem (1 = Greatest Influence; 3 = Least Influence):

Your Past	Your Mate's Past
____ Parents	____ Parents
____ Peers	____ Peers
____ Past in General	____ Past in General

2. Discuss why you ranked them as you did.

3. Complete this statement individually, then share it with your mate: "The one thing that would help me move beyond my past would be for you to . . ."

_____

_____

Make a date with your mate to meet in the next few days to complete **HomeBuilders Project #3**. This will aid you as a couple in the process of building one another's self-esteem. Your leader will ask you at the next session to share one thing from this experience.

Date	Time	Location

▪

Building Your Mate's Self-Esteem   by Dennis and Barbara Rainey

▪ "Helping Your Mate Clean Out the Attic of the Past" is the subject covered in chapter 6, pp. 82–101, in **Building Your Mate's Self-Esteem**. This will help you consider further the issues discussed in this session.

▪ Before your next session you will want to read chapter 7, pp. 103–114, in **Building Your Mate's Self-Esteem**. This chapter deals with the issue of "Words Are Seeds."

HomeBuilders Project #3

NOTE: "Helping Your Mate Clean Out the Attic of the Past" is the subject in chapter 6, pp. 82–101, in **Building Your Mate's Self-Esteem**. This chapter contains very helpful advice for helping your mate and will help you consider further the issues discussed here.

As a Couple—5–10 Minutes

Introduction: Approach this project with caution. Perhaps no area of our lives haunts us more than our past with the mistakes we or others have made. If you are in doubt about sharing something with your mate, it would be advisable to seek wise counsel before doing so. One further word: different marriages have grown to different levels of maturing love, acceptance, and trust. The best advice for a project like this is to share what needs to be discussed and "put your mate's past behind." Never pry, and avoid unpleasant details except where it is absolutely necessary.

NOTE: It may be necessary to seek outside counseling if there are substantial issues that cannot be, or should not be, dealt with in this context.

If sensitive areas are exposed when discussing the past, never use these "failures" to punish your mate further—usually there has already been punishment enough. Remember: "Perfect love casts out all fear" (1 John 4:18a).

Individually—25–30 Minutes

Choose *one* of the three areas we previously discussed. Check the appropriate box for the area with which you would like to deal, then go to the section of this project dealing with that area. You and your mate may each choose different areas.

☐ Parents (Section 1)

☐ Peers (Section 2)

☐ Past in general (Section 3)

SECTION 1
PARENTS

1. Describe your home and family when you were growing up. What words come to mind?

_____

_____

_____

2. As parents, what did your mom and dad do best?

DAD	MOM
a.	a.
b.	b.
c.	c.

3. What did they not do well?

DAD	MOM
a.	a.
b.	b.
c.	c.

4. Describe your relationship with each of your parents. What are your fondest memories? What would you change? Describe the impact each has had on you.

DAD	MOM
a.	a.
b.	b.
c.	c.

5. Describe the emotions you feel toward each of your parents.

DAD	MOM
a.	a.
b.	b.
c.	c.

6. Do you presently hold any bitterness, resentment, or unresolved anger toward either or both of your parents? Please explain.

_____

_____

7. If you feel that you are holding something against your parents, why not take time right now to write out a statement of how you feel and then confess that resentment to God as sin?

_____

_____

_____

_____

If either or both of your parents are still living, please complete questions 8 and 9.

8. What action do you need to take toward your parents? A phone call, a letter, a meeting to confess and seek forgiveness?

_____

_____

9. List something you will do in the next 12 months to communicate honor to your parents. (See Dennis and Barbara Rainey's "Tributes" to their parents on pp. 60–63 as an example of giving honor.)

_____

_____

Dennis's Tribute

She's More Than Somebody's Mom*

When she was 35, she carried him in her womb. It wasn't easy being pregnant in 1948. There were no dishwashers or Pampers®, and there were only crude washing machines. After nine long months, he was finally born. Breech. A difficult, dangerous birth. She still says, "He came out feet first, hit the floor running, and he's been running ever since." Affectionally she calls him "The Roadrunner."

A warm kitchen was her trademark—the most secure place in the home—a shelter in the storm. Her narrow but tidy kitchen always attracted a crowd. It was the place where food and friends were made! She was a good listener. She always seemed to have the time.

Certain smells used to drift out of that kitchen—the aroma of a juicy cheeseburger drew him like a magnet. There were green beans seasoned with hickory smoked bacon grease. Sugar cookies. Pecan pie. And the best of all, chocolate bon-bons.

Oh, she wasn't perfect. Once when, as a mischievous three-year-old, he was banging pans together, she impatiently threw a pencil at him while she was on the phone. The pencil, much to her shock, narrowly missed his eye and left a sliver of lead in his cheek . . . it's still there. Another time she tied him to his bed because, when he was five years old, he tried to murder his teen-aged brother by throwing a gun at him. It narrowly missed his brother, but hit her prized antique vase instead.

* Also published in *Pulling Weeds and Planting Seeds* (San Bernardino, CA: Here's Life Publishers, 1989.

She taught him forgiveness too. When he was a teenager she forgave him when he got angry and took a swing at her (and fortunately missed). The most profound thing she modeled was a love for God and people. Compassion was always her companion. She taught him about giving to others even when she didn't feel like it. She also taught him about accountability, truthfulness, honesty, and transparency. She modeled a tough loyalty to his dad. He always knew divorce was never an option. And she took care of her own parents when old age took its toll. She also went to church . . . faithfully. In fact, she led this six-year-old boy to Jesus Christ in her Sunday evening Bible study class.

Even today, her age doesn't stop her from fishing in a cold rain, running off to get Chinese food, or "wolfing down" a cheeseburger and a dozen bon-bons with her son.

She's truly a woman to be honored. She's more than somebody's mother . . . she's my mom. "Mom, I love you."

—Dennis

Barbara's Tribute

One of my most vivid and pleasant memories is of us kids watching you both work and working with you. As I look back, much of the work I remember was seasonal. With Mom I remember weeding, working, and planting flower beds in the spring. Dad supervised us when he took down storm windows, and we kids got the screens, lined them up against tree trunks to be washed, rinsed, and hung in anticipation of the warm summer days to come. In the summer, there was flower-bed maintenance and lawn work to do. I remember my job was to trim the edges of the driveway and sidewalks with the hand clippers. When fall arrived there were leaves to be raked and storm windows to be returned to their protective duty. And then, as the snows came, our shovels kept the sidewalks and driveway clean.

There were inside duties as well—like cleaning sinks and learning to wash dishes the right way. Mom taught me to sew, iron, embroider and to finish what I started. I remember being told more than once, "Anything worth doing is worth doing well." Thank you for the gift of a strong work ethic from both experience and your example.

The gifts of character and common sense are now mine because of your model. I learned to value honesty, respect for my elders, and good manners. You taught me to be conservative and not wasteful, and to value quality because it would endure.

I'm thankful to you both for the gift of self-confidence. Though my self-esteem faltered during my teen years, you demonstrated that you trusted me and I always knew you believed in me. I remember your allowing me to do a lot with Jimmy when he was a baby and toddler. I felt at times like he was mine as I fed him, rocked him, talked and played with him, and took him to a carnival when he was three with my date.

You also expressed trust by allowing me to express my creativity—at your expense! You let me decorate the house at Christmas, arrange flowers in the summer, and fix my room up the way I wanted. But the one that takes the cake is when you let me paint the bathroom fire-engine red with white and black trim —a thing I don't think I'd let my kids do. But I'm very grateful for that expression of trust, because it gave me a greater sense of self-confidence.

Another priceless gift was the gift of a good spiritual foundation. As we faithfully attended church and Sunday school as a family, and as I was encouraged to attend Vacation Bible School in the summers and youth group in the teen years, I learned the central importance of God in my life. Because we were always there, I memorized many of the great Christian hymns which I love to this day.

Because you loved me you corrected my grammar, picked up my Kleenexes®, and you let me go: to France, to college, and to Dennis. Though many of the details are long since forgotten, I'll always remember how proud I felt as I walked down the aisle with dad, and you both gave me away in marriage.

The last gift I mention is in no way the least. In fact, it is probably the greatest because it is foundational to all the others. It is the example of your marriage. I cannot recall a single argument or disagreement between you. It was apparent that you loved each other, cared for each other, and liked each other. I never felt insecure or fearful that you would leave one another or get a divorce. I treasure that gift of your good, solid, happy marriage. I attribute a great deal of the success of my marriage to the example I saw in yours.

And so, in this the season of gift giving, some 38 years after you gave me the gift of life, I give you this tribute. With a heart of gratitude, I give you my appreciation, my admiration, and my love.

Your daughter, Barbara
Christmas 1987

Interact As a Couple—20–30 Minutes

1. Get back together with your mate and share your projects step by step. Don't condemn, just seek to understand where your mate is coming from. Be an active, sympathetic listener.

2. Finish by praying with and for your mate. Claim the truth of Philippians 3:13–14.

3. Close in prayer together praying aloud for each other.

Remember to bring your calendar for **MAKE A DATE** for your next session.

SECTION 2:
PEERS

Individually: 25–30 Minutes

1. Describe the impact that peers (past and present) have had on your self-esteem for good and bad.

Good	Bad

2. Growing up, what was the value system held by your peers?

_____

_____

3. How do peers today continue to challenge your values and convictions?

Positively	Negatively

4. Looking at your past relationships with peers, are there any incidents that you need to put behind you or people you need to forgive to put the past in perspective (Phil. 3:13–14)?

_____

_____

5. Are there any relationships with your peers where you are conforming to wrong values and thus not fulfilling God's standard for you (Romans 12:1–2)? If so, what are they and what do you need to do about it?

_____

_____

_____

Interact As a Couple: 20–30 Minutes

1. Get back together with your mate and go through each other's projects step by step. Don't condemn. Just seek to understand where your mate is coming from. Be an active listener.

2. Finish by praying with and for your mate. Ask God to "transform" you from the inside out according to Romans 12:2.

Remember to bring your calendar for **MAKE A DATE** to your next session.

SECTION 3
THE PAST IN GENERAL

Individually: 20–30 Minutes

1. Are there any incidents or areas from the past that continue to haunt or condemn you?

_____

_____

If so, how is the past continuing to affect you today?

_____

_____

2. List practical ways you think your mate can help you move beyond this.

_____

_____

3.　How do you need your mate to communicate to you so that you will feel accepted and not rejected?

_____

_____

4.　What does Romans 8:1 say about someone who has received Jesus Christ as Savior and Lord?

_____

How can your mate help you apply that truth to your life?

_____

_____

5.　Review the verses studied in Section B, "Putting the Past in Perspective."

6.　What are practical ways that you can help one another today to avoid spiritual compromise in your marriage? List at least three.

a. _____

_____

b. _____

_____

c. _____

_____

Interact As a Couple: 20–30 Minutes

1. Get back together with your mate and go through each other's project, step by step. Don't condemn. Just seek to understand where your mate is coming from. Be an active listener.

2. Finish by praying with and for your mate. Look up 1 John 1:9, 2 Corinthians 5:17, and 2 Corinthians 5:21. Pray these verses back to God. Claim them as true in your life and thank Him by faith for what He has taught you about your past.

Remember to bring your calendar for **MAKE A DATE** to your next session.

The words you speak to your mate have the potential to strengthen or poison your mate's self-esteem.

STRENGTHENING SELF-ESTEEM

	ACCEPTING UNCONDITIONALLY	PUTTING THE PAST IN PERSPECTIVE	**PLANTING POSITIVE WORDS**
LAW OF GIVING	LAW OF UNDERSTANDING	LAW OF SOWING AND REAPING	LAW OF DIVINE SUFFICIENCY

THE FOUNDATION

1.   Begin this session by sharing one thing you learned from **HomeBuilders Project #3**.

2.   List four or five of the most descriptive words or phrases about yourself. Your leader will randomly read these out loud and everyone will guess who is being described.

a. _____   c. _____

b. _____   d. _____

e. _____

NOTE: Notice how words have the ability to paint a picture about a person in another's mind.

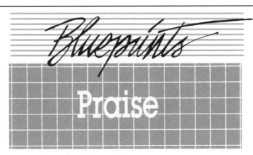

A. The Power of Words

1. "Sticks and stones may break my bones, but words will never hurt me." We're all familiar with this childhood saying. Comment on the accuracy or inaccuracy of this saying as you see it as an adult.

_____

_____

2. Think back on the power of words in your life. While growing up what were some statements made about you that you can still remember? Who said them? (Try to think of positive words as well as negative words. Which category is easier to remember? Why?) What effects did these words have on you?

_____

_____

3. Now let's look into the Scriptures and see how the power of words is described.

Proverbs 11:9 _____

_____

Proverbs 18:21_____

_____

71

Proverbs 12:25 _____

_____

Ephesians 4:29 _____

_____

4. Ecclesiastes 12:11 says, "The words of the wise are like goads, their collected sayings like firmly embedded nails given by one Shepherd." A goad (a long pointed stick used to prod sheep) *directs,* and a nail *secures.* How can your words "direct" and "secure" your mate's self-esteem? (Be specific.)

_____

_____

5. If possible, recall some of the words you used to affirm your mate during your courtship. What was the effect of those words upon your mate, your relationship, and you? (It may be appropriate for you both to write down the impact of those words on your lives.)

_____

_____

6. After having been married for a while, why is there a tendency to become callous or insensitive to the effects that words have on your mate? How can understanding the power of words begin to change your vocabulary with your mate?

_____

_____

7. Words can be likened to seeds, and seeds take time to sprout. What encouragement and hope does Galatians 6:9 give for diligently sowing good words in your mate? What's the warning here also?

_____

_____

Since words must be used carefully and constructively in building self-esteem, let's consider how best to speak rightly to your mate.

B. The Power of Praise

> **HomeBuilders Principle #6: Praise is the lubricant of relationships. It reduces friction and increases wear.**

1. Why do many people find it difficult to give or receive praise?

_____

_____

2. In what ways (methods) can you praise your mate?

_____

_____

3. For what character qualities can you give your mate praise?

_____

_____

(to be completed as a couple)

It is important to praise your mate specifically. Fill out at least three of the following statements. (Be specific.) Then share them with your mate.

a. "I appreciate you because . . ."

_____

_____

b. "I admire you for your . . ."

_____

_____

c. "Thank you for . . ."

_____

_____

d. "I feel confident that you can . . ."

_____

_____

e. "You made me feel loved when . . ."

_____

_____

f. "I like being with you because . . ."

_____

_____

g. "You're the best I know at . . ."

_____

_____

h. "I think you're growing in . . ."

_____

_____

Share with your mate how you felt while giving praise:

_____

_____

Share with your mate how you felt while receiving praise:

_____

_____

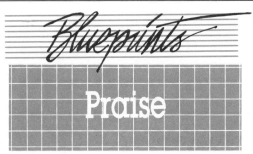

4. For your mate's praise to be effective, wise, and truthful you need to communicate when and how best to praise you. When do you most need to be praised? What's the best method for your mate to use on you (letter, note, hug, phone call, etc.)?

_____

_____

5. It is important that you be generous in praising your mate. The following are three areas where you can be generous in praise: encouragement, appreciation, and expressing belief in your mate. What type of statements—

a. encourage you? _____

_____

b. communicate you are appreciated? _____

_____

c. express belief to you? _____

_____

76

6. Read Ephesians 4:29. Then, while thinking of the earlier discussion on praise, share either:

■ one practical application you can use for your own marriage; or

■ one thing you praised about your mate (in **CONSTRUCTION** section).

_____

_____

Do not let any unwholesome talk come out of your mouths, but only what is helpful for building others up according to their needs, that it may benefit those who listen (Ephesians 4:29).

7. Conclude this time in prayer, thanking God for the praiseworthy qualities of your mate.

Make a date with your mate to meet in the next few days to complete **HomeBuilders Project #4**. Your leader will ask you at the next session to share one thing from this experience.

Date	Time	Location

▪

Recommended Reading

Building Your Mate's Self-Esteem   by Dennis and Barbara Rainey

■ "Words Are Seeds" is the subject covered in chapter 7, pp. 102–112, in **Building Your Mate's Self-Esteem**. This will help you consider further the issues discussed in this session.

■ Before your next session you will want to read chapter 9, pp. 124–137, in **Building Your Mate's Self-Esteem**. This chapter deals with the issue of "Down But Not Out for the Count."

As A Couple—5-10 Minutes

Review the previous session and share what was most helpful to you.

Individually—35-40 Minutes

1. List some words and phrases that you plant in your mate's life that produce:

WEEDS	FRUIT
a.	a.
b.	b.
c.	c.
d.	d.
e.	e.
f.	f.

80

2. Are there any "weed seeds" you've planted in your mate's life for which you need to ask forgiveness?

_____

_____

3. What are some words or phrases which bring you down and discourage you?

　　a. _____　　　d. _____

　　b. _____　　　e. _____

　　c. _____　　　f. _____

4. What are some words which encourage you and lift your spirit?

　　a. _____　　　d. _____

　　b. _____　　　e. _____

　　c. _____　　　f. _____

5. Complete the following sentences with one or more conclusions.

a. My mate can express belief in me by _____

_____

_____

_____

b. My mate can encourage me when I'm discouraged by _____

_____

_____

_____

6. Complete one of the following:

a. Write a paragraph or a letter of positive words to your mate. Pick one of the choices listed below:

▪ a letter of praise

▪ a letter of appreciation

▪ a letter of encouragement

▪ a letter stating your belief in your mate

b. Write a letter telling how you need your mate as a:

▪ woman/man

▪ homemaker/provider

▪ spiritual counterpart

▪ wife/husband

▪ mother/father

▪ lover

▪ friend

NOTE: When you write, be specific—avoid generalities.

As you write this letter, be sure to express your unconditional love and acceptance for your mate. Why not start by thinking of two or three important times you have had together. NOTE: Be vulnerable and transparent in your letter. If this is difficult, let him know at the beginning of the letter. Your mate will respect your openness even more.

(Use the following blank page to write your letter.)

Interact As a Couple—No Time Limit

Looking into each other's eyes, read your letter to your mate. Make mental notes of how your mate responds when you read yours and how you feel while listening to your mate read. This kind of project can be repeated over and over and over . . .

Remember to bring your calendar for **MAKE A DATE** for your next session.

_____

_____

_____

_____

_____

_____

_____

_____

_____

_____

_____

_____

_____

_____

_____

_____

_____

_____

_____

*Help your mate learn to separate
self-worth from performance by giving
your mate the freedom to risk failing.*

STRENGTHENING SELF-ESTEEM

	ACCEPTING UNCONDITIONALLY	PUTTING THE PAST IN PERSPECTIVE	PLANTING POSITIVE WORDS	**FREEDOM TO RISK FAILING**
LAW OF GIVING	LAW OF UNDERSTANDING	LAW OF SOWING AND REAPING		LAW OF DIVINE SUFFICIENCY

THE FOUNDATION

85

1. Begin this session by sharing one thing you learned from **HomeBuilders Project #4**.

2. Answer one of the following and share it with your group:

a. If you knew you couldn't fail (and cost *were not* an issue), what are some things you have always dreamed of trying?

_____

_____

b. If appropriate, share either a dream that was dashed or a colossal failure.

_____

_____

3. In which of the two situations below do you find it easier to respond verbally, emotionally, and/or physically?

☐ When your mate succeeds?

☐ When your mate fails?

Why do you think that is true for you?

_____

_____

A. Impact of Failure

1. What are some failures that people experience?

_____

_____

2. What are some of the consequences of these failures? Why do we fear these failures?

_____

_____

3. When you were growing up, how was failure viewed in your family? What was the relationship between "success" and "self-worth" in your family? How does that affect you today?

_____

_____

4. How would a fear of failure in a person affect self-esteem? What types of behavior would be likely when a person has a fear of failure?

_____

_____

Before your mate can experience the freedom to risk failing, you and your mate need a correct perspective on failure.

B. Outlook on Failure

1. As a culture, we have developed a "success syndrome" that creates the mirage that only a "successful person" has worth and value. How does the Scripture respond to this philosophy? (1 Samuel 16:7)

_____

_____

2. How does the Scripture define ultimate success? (Matthew 6:33)

_____

_____

For the purpose of our study, we are going to look at failure in two different categories:

■ Failure that is sin (disobedience, lying, immorality, lust, greed, losing our temper, etc.)

■ Failure that is *not* sin (business loss, errors, car accident, misunderstanding, losing or forgetting something, etc.)

While all sin is failure, not all failure is sin!

We will take a brief look at sinful failure (which we have already considered in Session Three) to help us get a perspective on failures of any kind. We will then move into Section C (How to Give the Freedom to Risk Failing), focusing on failure that is not sin.

3. Review the parable of the prodigal son found in Luke 15:11–32.
a. What do we learn about the son's feelings of worth in the midst of his own failure? (v. 18, 19, 21)

_____

_____

b. What was the father's response to his son's failure? (v. 20, 22–24)

_____

_____

c. What does this parable illustrate about God's love and acceptance of you?

_____

_____

4. What is the lesson for you here in responding when your mate fails?

_____

_____

5. Remember, not all failures are sin. But when sin does occur, what additional perspective does 1 Peter 4:8 give? How can you practically apply this verse in your marriage?

_____

_____

C. How to Give Your Mate the Freedom to Risk Failing

> **HomeBuilders Principle #7: By giving the freedom to risk failing, you will help your mate begin to separate self-worth from performance.**

You have a crucial role in helping your mate risk failing in any endeavor. Failure is inevitable in life. No one ever "does it right" every time. All of us need our mates to give us perspective and to help us confront a challenge and deal with those painful times whether we have lost our keys or our job. The question is, "How do you respond when your mate faces failure?" During the remainder of this session we will look at five essential actions which will give your mate the freedom to risk failure and the strength to recover from it.

Action Step #1

Assure your mate of your commitment, loyalty, and love regardless of performance (1 John 4:18a).

Share how your mate can communicate this to you.

_____

_____

Action Step #2

Remind your mate that "Your worth is not in what you do, but in who you are." See Ephesians 1:13–14.

How can a person fail without being a failure?

_____

_____

How can you send a clear message when your mate fails that "You are not a failure!"

_____

_____

Action Step #3

Comfort your mate with the truth: "God is in control" (Romans 8:28). Share an incident in which God brought "good" out of failure.

_____

_____

Action Step #4

Join with your mate in giving thanks in all things (1 Thessalonians 5:18).

Why is giving thanks to God an important part of dealing with failure?

_____

_____

Action Step #5

Encourage your mate not to lose heart when failure occurs (Proverbs 24:16; Galatians 6:9).

What are things your mate can say or do that encourage you to persevere?

_____

_____

_____

_____

(to be completed as a couple)

1. Which of the five "action steps" studied in this session does your mate do best? Give an example.

_____

_____

2. Which of the five actions do you need to do more of to help your mate?

_____

_____

1. How could you apply the previous five action steps above to help when your mate:

a. is habitually late?

_____

_____

b. repeatedly avoids decision making?

_____

_____

c. doesn't believe he or she can do it and doesn't risk?

_____

_____

d. takes a foolish risk?

_____

_____

2. What is one thing your mate does that communicates to you a freedom to risk failing?

_____

_____

3. What hope do we gain from:

a. Jude 24, 25?

_____

_____

b. This quote by Woodrow Wilson:

"It is better to fail in a cause that will ultimately succeed, than to succeed in a cause that will ultimately fail."

_____

_____

> HomeBuilders Principle #8: When you give your mate the freedom to risk failing, failure can become a tutor and not a judge.

4. Discuss **HomeBuilders Principle #8** and share the most meaningful thing you have learned from this session.

Make a date with your mate to meet together to complete **HomeBuilders Project #5**. Your leader will ask you at the next session to share one thing from this time together.

Date	Time	Location

■

Building Your Mate's Self-Esteem   by Dennis and Barbara Rainey

■ "Down But Not Out for the Count" is the subject covered in chapter 9, pp. 124–137, in **Building Your Mate's Self-Esteem**. This will help you consider further the issues discussed in this session.

■ Before your next session you will want to read chapter 13, pp. 176–187, in **Building Your Mate's Self-Esteem**. This chapter deals with the issue of "Getting the Ice off Your Balloon."

■

As a Couple—20–25 Minutes

Review Session Five and the Construction Project.

Individually—25–30 Minutes

1. List below a couple of times when you either failed or felt like a failure.

_____

_____

_____

What effect did these times have on you?

_____

_____

2. Does the fear of failing ever "drive" you? If so, in what ways and circumstances, and how?

_____

_____

3. How can your mate discern you are being driven by your fear of failure?

_____

_____

4. Where do you fear failing the most? Circle your top three.

a. At work   e. In a new venture

b. With the kids   f. Emotionally

c. With my mate   g. With friends

d. In finances   h. _____

5. How do your unreal expectations in each of the above areas contribute to your fear of failure?

_____

_____

6. Do you feel your mate gives you the freedom to fail? In what ways?

_____

_____

7. Is procrastination ever your response to the fear of failing? If so, how? How can your mate help you?

_____

_____

8. How does 1 Peter 4:8 relate to your failures and your mate's failures?

_____

_____

9. Look over the five actions below and place a star (•) by two or three you feel you need the most from your mate. Beside each one that has a star, write out some practical, tangible ways your mate can do that action for you.

a. Assure you of his or her commitment, loyalty, and love regardless of performance.

_____

_____

_____

b. Remind you that "Your worth is not in what you do, but in who you are."

_____

_____

_____

c. Comfort you with the truth, "God is in control."

_____

_____

_____

d. Join with you in giving thanks in all things.

_____

_____

_____

e. Encourage you not to lose heart when failure occurs.

_____

_____

_____

Interact As a Couple—15-20 Minutes

1. Go through your individual sections together.

2. Pray together. Thank God that He gives you the freedom to fail. Thank Him that by the power of the Holy Spirit, you and your mate can express the same freedom to each other.

Remember to bring your calendar for **MAKE A DATE** to your next session.

The HomeBuilders

C O U P L E S   S E R I E S

"Unless the Lord builds the house,
they labor in vain who build it."
Psalm 127:1

Help your mate keep life manageable and under the control of the Holy Spirit.

STRENGTHENING SELF-ESTEEM

KEEPING LIFE MANAGEABLE	ACCEPTING UNCONDITIONALLY	PUTTING THE PAST IN PERSPECTIVE	PLANTING POSITIVE WORDS	FREEDOM TO RISK FAILING
LAW OF GIVING	LAW OF UNDERSTANDING	LAW OF SOWING AND REAPING	LAW OF DIVINE SUFFICIENCY	

THE FOUNDATION

1. Begin this session by sharing what you learned from **HomeBuilders Project #5**.

2. a. What time of the year is the most pressured for you and your family?

_____

_____

   b. How does this pressure usually affect you?

_____

_____

3. How does comparison with others put pressure on you, your mate, and your family?

_____

_____

A. A Description of the Problem

1. a. Why do you think that dealing with pressure is such a relevant topic for married people today?

_____

_____

b. How does pressure relate to the topic of self-esteem?

_____

_____

2. Rank the top three factors which contribute most pressure for you and your mate.

ME	MY MATE	
☐	☐	Unrealistic expectations
☐	☐	Failure to make tough decisions
☐	☐	Tendency to let others decide
☐	☐	Comparisons with our culture
☐	☐	Comparisons with Christian community
☐	☐	Procrastination
☐	☐	Overcommitment
☐	☐	Job demands
☐	☐	Change
☐	☐	Unresolved conflict with a child or parent

☐ ☐ Financial pressures
☐ ☐ Unexpected problems
☐ ☐ Recurring interpersonal friction
☐ ☐ Uncertain future
☐ ☐ Health Problems
☐ ☐ In-laws
☐ ☐ Friends
☐ ☐ Church involvement
☐ ☐ Other _____

3. Share with the group your top three factors and how they affect you.

4. How is there additional pressure in the life of a Christian?

_____

_____

5. a. Is pressure good or bad? Why?

_____

_____

b. Discuss the following quote by J. Hudson Taylor, missionary to China: "It matters not how *great* the pressure is, only *where* the pressure lies. If we make sure it never comes *between* us and our Lord, then the greater the pressure, the more it presses us to *Him*."

_____

_____

B. How to Help Your Mate Handle Pressure

1. Be Wise

Your real priorities are determined by the choices you make each day. These choices are a reflection of your values. Your calendar and checkbook are two reflections of your priorities and thus your values.

a. One of the shortcomings of couples today is that we do not take the necessary time to discuss as a couple what our values are. A couple's priorities will be a reflection of their real values. When a couple does not clarify what is truly important the tendency is to live a hurried lifestyle which can ultimately end up as a wasted life.

Ephesians 5:15-17 gives us three exhortations for coming to grips with priorities and ultimately our values.

(1) What three things does Ephesians 5:15-17 teach us about being wise and determining our priorities?

(a) _____

(b) _____

(c) _____

(2) How can understanding each of these three exhortations help you handle pressure? Apply each of these three in handling pressure.

(a) _____

(b) _____

(c) _____

b. In order to apply this principle successfully, you must be wise. Wisdom is godly skill in everyday living; living life according to God's design; being obedient to His laws, commandments, and Word.

(1) If you need wisdom to resolve pressures of a hurried life, what help does James 1:2-8 offer?

_____

_____

(2) As a couple, how have you and your mate used prayer to gain skill in everyday living in a pressurized society?

_____

_____

(3) Many couples seldom pray together. Why is prayer sometimes uncomfortable for a couple?

_____

_____

HomeBuilders Principle #9: Through prayer we can ask God for wisdom, which will enable us as a couple to handle the pressures of life.

(to be completed as a couple)

Check one or two of the following areas of walking wisely which you and your mate can discuss this week to help each other do (v. 15).

☐ Take a look at your mate's job and work schedule to see if a better balance can be reached with the demands of home.

☐ If appropriate, discuss how your children may be contributing pressure to your mate's life. Develop a game plan for beginning to solve the problem.

☐ Schedule a monthly planning session to help your mate keep the calendar balanced (review the next 30, 90, and 180 days).

☐ With your mate's permission, talk about what's really important to each of you.

☐ List all present commitments and activities that you, your mate, and family are committed to and make adjustments.

☐ Help your mate practice saying "No" once a day.

☐ Talk about a time of the year that tends to torpedo you as a couple and formulate an offensive game plan for anticipating the hectic pace of that particular time.

☐ Pray together—"When is the best time for us to pray together?"

☐ Other _____

In the space provided below commit in writing to a plan to accomplish that which you have previously discussed.

_____

_____

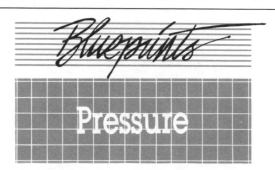

2. Be Filled

a. Ephesians 5:18 exhorts us to be filled with the Holy Spirit. What does it mean to be filled with the Holy Spirit?

_____

_____

b. Why is it many Christians are driven by the culture, by insecurity, or by the demands of others, and not directed and empowered by the Holy Spirit?

_____

_____

c. How does being filled with the Holy Spirit affect self-esteem? (Hebrews 11:6, Galatians 5:22,23)

_____

_____

d. How could you encourage your mate to be empowered by the Holy Spirit?

_____

_____

e. What advice would you give to the person whose mate **does not desire** to be filled with the Holy Spirit?

_____

_____

HomeBuilders Principle #10: The Holy Spirit is God's personal provision for discerning His direction, and bringing peace and order to your life, marriage, and family.

---

3. Be Subject

a. Read Ephesians 5:21. What does it mean to "be subject" to one another?

_____

_____

b. How can accountability (being subject) to each other protect or preserve you and your mate from becoming overcommitted or feeling too much pressure?

_____

_____

c. Why don't individuals within marriage want to be held accountable to each other?

_____

_____

> HomeBuilders Principle #11: Accountability between husband and wife is the anchor that God has given to us for finding security, protection, and balance in the storms of life.

d. What are some practical areas in which you and your mate need to deal with pressure by becoming accountable to each other?

_____

_____

SUMMARY: EPHESIANS 5:15–21
Be Wise
■ Help your mate schedule time to reflect his or her values.
■ Protect your mate's time for thought and prayer.
■ Determine your bottom-line values—where are you unwilling to fail?
Be Filled
■ Determine to be led by the Spirit, not driven by the culture, by insecurity, or by the demands of others.
■ Practice Spiritual Breathing:
Exhale: Confess your sin to God (1 John 1:9) Inhale: Be filled with the Spirit (Ephesians 5:18)
■ Nurture the Fruit of the Spirit (Galatians 5:22, 23).
■ Encourage your mate to be led by the Spirit.
Be Subject
■ Be accountable to one another for the use of your time.
■ Protect one another's time.
■ Help your mate make tough decisions and say "No" when necessary—but avoid "taking over."

Make a Date

Make a date with your mate to meet in the next few days to complete **HomeBuilders Project #6**. Your leader will ask you at the next session to share one thing from this experience.

| _____ | _____ | _____ |
| Date | Time | Location |

■

Recommended Reading

Building Your Mate's Self-Esteem   by Dennis and Barbara Rainey

■ "Getting the Ice off Your Balloon" is the subject covered in chapter 13, pp. 176–187, in **Building Your Mate's Self-Esteem**. This will help you consider further the issues discussed in this session.

■ HUSBANDS—Before your next session you will want to read chapter 15, pp. 202–219, in **Building Your Mate's Self-Esteem**. This chapter deals with the issue of "Five Investment Tips That Will Yield a Great Return."

WIVES—Before your next session you will want to read chapter 16, pp. 220–238, in **Building Your Mate's Self-Esteem**. This chapter deals with the issue of "Securing Your Man."

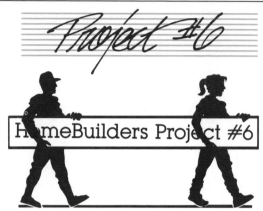

Individually—30–35 Minutes

1. Carefully evaluate your calendar, priorities, and checkbook. What values do they represent?

_____

_____

2. a. Right now, what is causing pressure in your life? List 3–5 items if possible.

(1) _____

(2) _____

(3) _____

(4) _____

(5) _____

b. What is causing pressure in your mate's life?

(1) _____

(2) _____

(3) _____

(4) _____

(5) _____

3. List the top five values you hold as important.

a. _____

b. _____

c. _____

d. _____

e. _____

4. Take a realistic look at your schedule (an average day—a typical week). List the top five activities other than sleeping that occupy the majority of your time.

a. _____

b. _____

c. _____

d. _____

e. _____

Interact As a Couple

1. Compare your answers from the individual section. Ask your mate "why" for each item he or she listed. Find out the reasons for his or her choices. Discuss your differences.

115

2. Compare your "values" lists with your "time" lists. Does your expenditure of time match your top five values? If not, why not?

_____

_____

3. Together, list all your activities from the individual section and categorize them into one of the following two areas.

Those We Can Control	Those We Cannot Control
_____	_____
_____	_____
_____	_____
_____	_____
_____	_____

4. What decisions need to be made about "Those We Can Control" to help your schedule more clearly reflect your values? Write out what you have decided.

Problem	Decision
_____	_____
	_____
_____	_____
	_____
_____	_____
	_____

5. Together, decide on some specific ways each of you can help the other maintain a balanced lifestyle. List those ideas below.

_____

_____

_____

_____

6. Read Matthew 11:28–30 together. Discuss what the Lord means and promises as He says, "Come . . . take . . . and learn from Me." What message is there here for our hectic lifestyles?

_____

_____

7. Pull out your calendars and schedule a weekly planning time that would help you apply these principles. Close your time in prayer by asking for wisdom.

Remember to bring your calendar for **MAKE A DATE** to your next session.

The HomeBuilders

C O U P L E S   S E R I E S

"Unless the Lord builds the house,
they labor in vain who build it."
Psalm 127:1

As a husband, your primary responsibility is to love your wife and help her develop into the woman God made her to be.

STRENGTHENING SELF-ESTEEM

	HUSBAND: INVEST IN YOUR WIFE	WIFE: BUILD HIS SECURITY		
KEEPING LIFE MANAGEABLE	ACCEPTING UNCONDITIONALLY	PUTTING THE PAST IN PERSPECTIVE	PLANTING POSITIVE WORDS	FREEDOM TO RISK FAILING
LAW OF GIVING	LAW OF UNDERSTANDING	LAW OF SOWING AND REAPING	LAW OF DIVINE SUFFICIENCY	

THE FOUNDATION

1. Begin this session by sharing one thing you learned from **HomeBuilders Project #6**.

2. Choose one of the following:

a. What are the needs women have today in building a healthy self-esteem?

_____

_____

b. In what area(s) have you succeeded in building your wife's self-esteem?

_____

_____

c. Where do you struggle the most with building your wife's self-esteem?

_____

_____

HomeBuilders Principle #12: God has appointed you as the husband to build your wife's self-esteem.

A. Treat Her As a Participating Partner

1. Peter writes in 1 Peter 3:7 that husbands are to treat their wives as "fellow heir(s) of the grace of life." What comes to your mind when you think of a *fully* participating partner?

_____

_____

2. List below three to five ways you need your wife. Share at least one with the group.

_____

_____

_____

_____

_____

3. Why do you think it is difficult for a man to admit verbally his need for his wife as his partner? Why is it difficult for you?

_____

_____

4. What are some specific ways you can communicate to your wife your need for her?

_____

_____

5. How does showing your need for your wife build her self-esteem?

_____

_____

B. Protect Her

1. 1 Peter 3:7 also says to "live with your wife in an understanding way, as with a weaker vessel, since she is a woman." This Scripture touches on your wife's need for security and protection. How has your wife revealed to you her need to feel protected by you?

_____

_____

2. Check one or more of the "emotional muggers" listed below which take advantage of your wife and rob her of her sense of value, joy, and confidence:

☐ Overscheduling   ☐ Manipulation by others

☐ Unrealistic goals or expectations   ☐ Comparisons with others

☐ Burnout at   ☐ Demands of children/teens
    work/church/school/home

☐ Discouragement in people   ☐ Physical (health/appearance)

☐ _____   ☐ _____

3. Share one or two practical ways you can protect your wife from the above "muggers" without overprotecting her or stifling her creativity as a person.

_____

_____

C. Honor Her

1. 1 Peter 3:7 exhorts the husband to "grant her honor." What are some ways you can communicate respect and honor for your wife?

_____

_____

2. What are some ways husbands can communicate disrespect and lack of honor to their wives?

_____

_____

3. One way of honoring is to "compete" for your wife—to continue to "court" her, showing her she is important to you. Share some ideas of how you compete for your wife and add romance to your relationship.

_____

_____

_____

4. Another way of honoring is to speak respectfully of her for who she is and all that she accomplishes. Share one or two examples of how you honor your wife by what you say. How can you do a better job of this?

_____

_____

5. What are some common courtesies which are overlooked today that may need to be revived?

_____

_____

D. Develop Her Gifts and Horizons As a Woman

1. Read Ephesians 5:28, 29. Discuss what it means practically to "nourish" and "cherish" our wives.

_____

_____

2. How can a husband help his wife to grow (nourish) and to feel valued (cherished) in each of the following areas?

a. Spiritual growth

_____

_____

b. Gifts, talents, and abilities

_____

_____

c. Dreams and visions for the future

_____

_____

3. Why do we as men tend to neglect nourishing and cherishing our wives?

_____

_____

E. Assist in Problem Solving

1. List three to five areas where your wife is currently facing problems, and put a star by those that are recurring problems.

_____

_____

_____

_____

2. Discuss what lessons you've learned in working with your wife at solving problems.

_____

_____

3. What one problem, if solved, would greatly encourage and strengthen your wife's self-esteem?

_____

_____

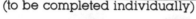

(to be completed individually)

Review all five tips. Now pick one of your wife's areas of greatest need and select one or two actions to take this week. Write a description of a practical way you will do each one. CAUTION: DO NOT CHOOSE AN EASY WAY OUT!

Write down one or two actions which will really help her—demonstrate your love for her.

_____

_____

_____

_____

Conclude your time by reading the following verses and praying together, asking God to help you strengthen your wife as she runs the race of life:

Therefore, since we have so great a cloud of witnesses
    surrounding us,
  let us also lay aside every encumbrance,
    and the sin which so easily entangles us,
  and let us run with endurance the race that is set before us,
    fixing our eyes on Jesus,
      the author and perfecter of faith,

who for the joy set before Him endured the cross, despising
the shame,
and has sat down at the right hand of the throne of God.
For consider Him who has endured such hostility by sinners
against Himself,
so that you may not grow weary and lose heart (Hebrews
12:1– 3).

Make a date with your mate to meet in the next few days to complete **HomeBuilders Project #7**. Your leader will ask you at the next session to share one thing from this experience.

Date	Time	Location

■

Building Your Mate's Self-Esteem   by Dennis and Barbara Rainey

■ "Five Investment Tips That Will Yield a Great Return" is the subject covered in chapter 15, pp. 202–219, in **Building Your Mate's Self-Esteem**. This will help you consider further the issues discussed in this session.

■ Before your next session you will want to read chapter 14, pp. 188–201, in **Building Your Mate's Self-Esteem**. This chapter deals with the issue of "Leaving a Legacy That Will Outlive You."

■

As a Couple—10-15 Minutes

1. Share what each of you discussed and learned from the session you just completed.

2. Review each of your **CONSTRUCTION** sections and share one of two actions you intend to take.

Individually—15-20 Minutes

Imagine you have just received the following letter from your wife. How would you respond in writing? Use the sheet of "stationery" on page 132 to write your response. (Be specific, and express how you feel.)

My dearest husband . . .

Thank you for choosing me to share your life with you. Thank you for your honesty and transparency. I know it can be painful at times.

Deep down inside I really know that you love me. But I'm a woman and I need tangible reminders of your love. There is very little in this life of greater value to me than your love. I need it. I need you.

Could I ask a favor? I love to receive letters from you, but I don't ever want to ask for them . . . it takes all the fun out of receiving them if it's my idea. But would you write me a letter?

I need to know:

- how you appreciate me . . .
- what I've done to show that I respect you . . .
- how I've been an encouragement to you . . .
- that you appreciate the "little things" I do every week for you . . .
- of your unconditional acceptance, just as I am (Is it there? I need to know) . . .
- how I am a partner with you . . .
- why you enjoy me . . .
- what you like about me . . .
- how I've changed for good or ways that you've seen me grow (I forget sometimes) . . .
- that you want to lead me and do what is best for me . . .
- that you want to meet my needs . . .
- that your love will persevere.

You can write it any way you'd like, but please tell me. I really do respect you.

I love you,
your wife

P.S.   I'm not perfect either, but I'm glad we're in this thing together.

131

Wife Builder's Inventory

The following questions will help you "inventory" your most valuable friend, your wife. By making yourself answer these questions periodically, you maintain your protection of her and thus build her self-esteem.

1. a. What is the pace of her life?

_____

_____

b. Does my schedule cause her more problems than it does me? How does it affect her?

_____

_____

c. Does my schedule allow for any breathers for her? For us? What do I need to do differently?

_____

_____

2. a. What kind of pace can she keep? For how long?

_____

_____

b. What does she need after an intensely busy or difficult period of time?

_____

_____

3. a. What tends to crush her? What pops her balloon?

_____

_____

    b. What causes her to feel she is failing?

_____

_____

    c. What can I do about it?

_____

_____

4. a. What decisions do I need to make that will reduce pressure or break up a log jam?

_____

_____

    b. Am I putting off some things that, if I went ahead and did them, would facilitate her daily routine and thereby help her in the long run? If so, what?

_____

_____

5. What directions can I give her to protect her as she moves through a difficult period of time?

_____

_____

6. a. Does she need to be rescued for an evening? A weekend? An extended period? What should the agenda be for our time?

_____

_____

b. When can I carry her off for a romantic retreat just for us? How can I surprise her?

_____

_____

7. Read Ephesians 5:25–33 and answer the following questions.

a. How did Jesus Christ love the church?

_____

_____

b. How did He demonstrate sacrificial love?

_____

_____

c. How are you commanded to love your wife?

_____

_____

d. What happens when you love her this way?

_____

_____

8. After having completed the "Wife Builder's Inventory" and the study of Ephesians 5, list your three action points—the questions you need to ask your wife on the steps you need to take.

_____

_____

_____

9. Close by praying for your wife. Ask God to show you what it truly means to love her even as He loves us.

Interact As a Couple—15 Minutes

1. a. Ask your wife questions 1–5 as she shares her work with you.

b. Read her your answer to those same questions.

c. Pray together. Ask God to help you be a good steward of your wife. Thank Him for the opportunity He has entrusted you with to lead her.

Remember to bring your calendar for **MAKE A DATE** to your next session.

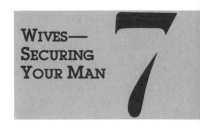

Your husband needs you to believe in him and support him in order to be secure as a man.

STRENGTHENING SELF-ESTEEM

	HUSBAND: INVEST IN YOUR WIFE	WIFE: BUILD HIS SECURITY		
KEEPING LIFE MANAGEABLE	ACCEPTING UNCONDITIONALLY	PUTTING THE PAST IN PERSPECTIVE	PLANTING POSITIVE WORDS	FREEDOM TO RISK FAILING
LAW OF GIVING	LAW OF UNDERSTANDING	LAW OF SOWING AND REAPING	LAW OF DIVINE SUFFICIENCY	

THE FOUNDATION

1. Begin this session by sharing one thing you learned from **HomeBuilders Project #6**.

2. Although most men appear outwardly secure, inwardly most are anxious and uncertain. Why do you think so many men today are insecure?

_____

_____

3. Choose one of the following and answer:

a. What would you say would be the top three ways to build a man's self-esteem?

_____

_____

b. In what area do you feel you've had some success in building your husband's self-esteem?

_____

_____

c. Why do you believe a wife is crucial to a husband's self-esteem?

_____

_____

4. If appropriate, reflect on how your mom did or did not build your dad's self-esteem.

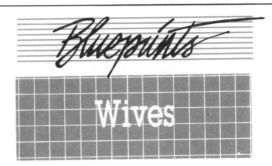

HomeBuilders Principle #13: Your husband's value and security as a man is most affected by you, his wife. You are the most important person in his life.

A. Respect His Personhood

1. As a group write your own definition of the word *respect*.

_____

_____

2. Read Ephesians 5:33b.

a. What does it mean to respect your husband?

_____

_____

139

b. Why do you think your husband needs your respect? How is it essential to his self-esteem?

_____

_____

3. In each of the following situations decide what a wife could do to demonstrate respect for her husband:

a. A dictatorial husband

_____

_____

b. A passive husband

_____

_____

c. Presenting him with a problem

_____

_____

d. Disagreeing with him on a decision

_____

_____

e. Dealing with a failure of his

_____

_____

f. Responding to his anger/disappointment/fear/or other unpleasant emotions

_____

_____

4. As a result of the discussion in the previous question, what are some creative ways in which you could show respect to your husband? What area will you focus on this week?

_____

_____

B. Understand His Manhood

1. Read Proverbs 24:3. How does understanding establish a solid relationship?

2. One of the major sources of misunderstanding in a marriage is the differences between men and women. How is your husband (as a man) different from you (as a woman) in the following five areas? Fill in the blanks on page 142 and circle the area in which there has been the greatest difference in your relationship with your husband.

141

Area	Man	Woman
PHYSICAL		
THINKING		
SEX		
COMMUNICATION		
PROBLEM SOLVING		

Discuss your observations on the chart above.

3. One of the areas that can cause stress in a marriage relationship is the different expressed desire for sex between husbands and wives. Many wives do not understand how their husband's sexual drive is tied to his self-esteem as a man.

a. In what ways do you think wives misunderstand their husbands in the sexual relationship?

_____

_____

b. Why is it important in a sexual relationship for a man to understand and meet his wife's emotional needs?

_____

_____

c. In light of this, what can a woman do to better meet her husband's physical needs?

_____

_____

d. What can a woman do to help her husband better meet her emotional needs?

_____

_____

e. How could understanding these differences help you respect your husband more?

_____

_____

f. How does understanding your husband establish and strengthen his self-esteem?

_____

_____

4. What one thing could you do or remember better to understand your husband as a man?

_____

_____

C. Adapt to Him and His Dreams

This session concludes with consideration of the importance of a woman's adapting to her husband. In 1 Peter 3:1-6, wives are commanded to adapt their lives to their husbands'. The word *submit* in the original Greek language is a military term which means "to arrange or rank under the authority of another."

Perhaps no other word than *submit* receives such a negative response from women today. However, it is clear from Scripture that for a man to become the secure, loving leader God intended him to be, he must have a wife who not only believes in him, but is willing to submit to him as well.

1. Read 1 Peter 3:1-6:

> (1) Wives, fit in with your husbands' plans; for then if they refuse to listen when you talk to them about the Lord, they will be won by your respectful, pure behavior. (2) Your godly lives will speak to them better than any words. (3) Don't be concerned about the outward beauty that depends on jewelry, or beautiful clothes, or hair arrangement. (4) Be beautiful inside, in your hearts, with the lasting charm of a gentle and quiet spirit which is so precious to God. (5) That kind of deep beauty was seen in the saintly women of old, who trusted God and fitted in with their husbands' plans. (6) Sarah, for instance, obeyed her husband Abraham, honoring him as head of the house. And if you do the same, you will be following in her steps like good daughters and doing what is right; then you will not need to fear (offending your husbands) (LB).

a. What does it mean to adapt or fit in with your husband's plans?

_____

_____

b. What does v. 5 say is the basis for a wife's ability to adapt to him?

_____

_____

c. How does our hope in God give us ability to adapt?

_____

_____

2. Why do some women struggle with adapting to their husbands?

_____

_____

3. What area in which you need to adapt to your husband is the one you find most important to his self-image?

_____

_____

4. How does adapting to him affect his self-esteem and ability to deal with:

a. A change of jobs/relocation?

_____

_____

b. A need to take leadership?

_____

_____

c. A financial risk/crisis?

_____

_____

d. Lack of maturity? ·

_____

_____

5. a. List ways you have adapted to your husband:

_____

_____

b. What was the result on his self-esteem?

_____

_____

6. What is the most important thing you have learned from this session?

_____

_____

_____

Construction

(to be completed individually)

Review each of the three areas in this session. Now select one or two actions you will take this week. Write out a description of a practical way you will do each one. CAUTION: DO NOT CHOOSE THE EASY WAY OUT!

_____

_____

_____

_____

Conclude your time by reading the following verses and praying together, asking God to help you strengthen your husband as he runs the race of life.

> Therefore, since we have so great a cloud of witnesses
>   surrounding us,
> let us also lay aside every encumbrance,
>   and the sin which so easily entangles us,
> and let us run with endurance the race that is set before us,
>   fixing our eyes on Jesus,
>   the author and perfecter of faith,
> who for the joy set before Him endured the cross, despising
>   the shame,
>   and has sat down at the right hand of the throne of God.
> For consider Him who has endured such hostility by sinners
>   against Himself,
>   so that you may not grow weary and lose heart (Hebrews
>   12:1– 3).

147

Make a date with your mate to meet in the next few days to complete **HomeBuilders Project #7**. Your leader will ask you at the next session to share one thing from this experience.

Date	Time	Location

■

Building Your Mate's Self-Esteem   by Dennis and Barbara Rainey

■ "Securing Your Man" is the subject covered in chapter 16, pp. 220–238, in **Building Your Mate's Self-Esteem**. This will help you consider further the issues discussed in this session.

■ Before your next session you will want to read chapter 14, pp. 188–201, in **Building Your Mate's Self-Esteem**. This chapter deals with the issue of "Leaving a Legacy That Will Outlive You."

HomeBuilders Project #7

As a Couple—10–15 Minutes

1. Share what each of you discussed and learned from the session you just completed.

_____

_____

2. Review each of your **CONSTRUCTION** sections and share one or two actions you intend to take.

_____

_____

Individually—20 Minutes

Answer the following:

1. a. Which of the following attitudes are the most difficult for you to demonstrate toward your husband? (Check the ones that apply.)

☐ Understanding his manhood _____

☐ Understanding his need for work _____

☐ Understanding his sexual need _____

☐ Giving him respect _____

☐ Adapting to him _____

☐ Sharing his dreams _____

    b. Next to each attitude that you checked above, tell why you struggle in that area.

    c. What can you do about this problem area? Pray? Change your focus? Something else?

_____

_____

2. a. What are your husband's dreams and goals? List as many as you can think of.

(1) _____   (6) _____

(2) _____   (7) _____

(3) _____   (8) _____

(4) _____   (9) _____

(5) _____   (10) _____

    b. How can you best encourage him to achieve these goals?

_____

_____

3. a. Are you willing for him to become and do all that God has planned? What do you fear the most? A move (near or far)? A change in your finances? A change in your job? Or the position you would be expected to fill as a result of your husband's position? Write down how you feel.

_____

_____

b. In prayer, give that area of fear and insecurity to God. Ask Him to free you from that personal concern so you will not be a hindrance to God's plan for your husband's life, but a true biblical helper.

_____

_____

4. What are your husband's positive character qualities? Is he compassionate, kind, and sensitive toward people? Is he disciplined and dedicated? Is he faithful and loyal, persevering in difficulties? Do the words *truthful, honest,* or *decisive* describe your mate? What are his talents and strengths? Make a list. Refresh your memory. Refurbish your respect.

List at least five positive character qualities that you respect and admire in your husband.

a. _____

b. _____

c. _____

d. _____

e. _____

Interact As a Couple—20-25 Minutes

1. Share with your husband what it is you admire and respect about him. Assure him that you trust his leadership.

Husbands: share your letter with your wife.

2. Wives: share with your husband the list you made of his dreams and goals. Circle the ones he indicates he feels strongly about. How "right on" are you? Assure him that you want to share those dreams and work toward those goals with him.

Remember to bring your calendar for **MAKE A DATE** to your next session.

Optional Project

(This project can be completed this weekend or saved for a later date.) Imagine you have received the following letter from your mate. How would you respond in writing? Use the sheet of "stationery" which follows the letter to write your response. Be specific, and express how you feel.

My dearest wife . . .

Thank you for choosing me to share your life with you. Thank you for your honesty and transparency. I know it can be painful at times.

Deep down inside I really know that you love me. But I need tangible reminders of your love. There is very little in this life of greater value to me than your love. I need it. I need you.

Could I ask a favor? I love to receive letters from you, but I don't ever want to ask for them . . . it takes all the fun out of receiving them if it's my idea. But would you write me a letter?

I need to know:

- how you appreciate me . . .
- what I've done to show that I respect you . . .
- how I've been an encouragement to you . . .
- that you appreciate the "little things" I do every week for you . . .
- of your unconditional acceptance, just as I am (Is it there? I need to know) . . .
- how I am a partner with you . . .
- why you enjoy me . . .
- what you like about me . . .
- how I've changed for good or ways that you've seen me grow (I forget sometimes) . . .
- that you want to submit to me and encourage me to reach my goals . . .
- that you want to meet my needs . . .
- that your love will persevere.

You can write it any way you'd like, but please tell me. I really

do respect you.   I love you,
                                                       Your husband

P.S.   I'm not perfect either, but I'm glad we're in this thing together.

True significance is found as a couple experience God's love and respond by investing themselves in the cause that will outlive them.

STRENGTHENING SELF-ESTEEM

DISCOVERING DIGNITY THROUGH DESTINY				
	HUSBAND: INVEST IN YOUR WIFE	WIFE: BUILD HIS SECURITY		
KEEPING LIFE MANAGEABLE	ACCEPTING UNCONDITIONALLY	PUTTING THE PAST IN PERSPECTIVE	PLANTING POSITIVE WORDS	FREEDOM TO RISK FAILING
LAW OF GIVING	LAW OF UNDERSTANDING	LAW OF SOWING AND REAPING	LAW OF DIVINE SUFFICIENCY	

THE FOUNDATION

1. Go through the following list of **HomeBuilders Principles**. Select the *top five* which you have found to be most helpful to you in building your mate's self-esteem and number them according to their value to you (1 = most valuable, 2 = second most valuable, etc.).

_____ **HomeBuilders Principle #1:** It is only as you help your mate understand the right value system, God's truth as found in the Scriptures, that you can help your mate slay the phantom and become who God wants him or her to be.

_____ **HomeBuilders Principle #2:** Everyone needs to be accepted by at least one other person—his or her mate.

_____ **HomeBuilders Principle #3:** It is only as your mate experiences the security of your unconditional love that he or she will risk being real in the marriage relationship.

_____ **HomeBuilders Principle #4:** It is imperative that you and your mate experience God's forgiveness through Christ if you are to put your pasts behind you and have hope for the future.

_____ **HomeBuilders Principle #5:** In dealing with your mate's past, it is far better to be kind and forgiving than condemning.

_____ **HomeBuilders Principle #6:** Praise is the lubricant of relationships. It reduces friction and increases wear.

_____ **HomeBuilders Principle #7:** By giving the freedom to fail you will help your mate begin to separate self-worth from performance.

_____ **HomeBuilders Principle #8:** When you give your mate the freedom to risk failing, failure can become a tutor and not a judge.

_____ **HomeBuilders Principle #9:** Through prayer we can ask God for wisdom, which will enable us as a couple to handle the pressures of life.

_____ **HomeBuilders Principle #10:** The Holy Spirit is God's personal provision for discerning His direction and bringing peace and order to your home.

_____ **HomeBuilders Principle #11:** Accountability between husband and wife is the anchor that God has given to us for finding security, protection, and balance in the storms of life.

_____ **HomeBuilders Principle #12:** God has appointed you as the husband to build your wife's self-esteem.

_____ **HomeBuilders Principle #13:** Your husband's value and security as a man is most affected by you, his wife. You are the most important person in his life.

2. Share one of the five and tell why you found it helpful.

3. What is one way your mate has helped build your self-esteem since this series began? (Be specific.)

_____

_____

_____

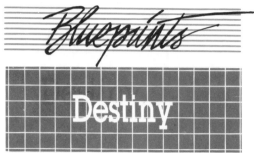

Our concluding session will focus on how you as a couple can maintain a healthy sense of self-esteem through determining and following God's direction for your lives. As you continue the lifetime process of clarifying God's direction for your lives together, you will discover the privilege of being a part of building an invisible eternal kingdom—the kingdom of God of which Jesus spoke so frequently.

A. What Is Our Need?

1. Why is a sense of destiny and direction important for an individual? For you?

_____

_____

2. Why is it that most couples do not evidence a sense of shared purpose, direction, and destiny?

_____

_____

3. Explain how a sense of "divine destiny" for a couple strengthens a marriage. How have you experienced this?

_____

_____

Each of us needs to realize that God has a plan (direction) for our lives, not only as individuals but also as couples. Up to this point, what has been the major purpose and direction for your marriage?

_____

_____

A Christian marriage which does not embrace a divine destiny has a distorted purpose, has no direction, or has an unclear focus. Marriages without God's direction are sitting ducks for temptation, mediocrity, and wasted lives. They experience less than God's best.

4. We feel that the items listed below are some of the most common "robbers" of what God has called us to do—they tend to "take away" our focus on God's direction for us. Which of the following pursuits tend to distract you most frequently from God's purpose? How?

☐ Material Goods/Comfort _____

☐ Money _____

☐ Accomplishments/Success _____

☐ Recognition _____

☐ Pleasure _____

☐ Uncertainty about God's purpose _____

☐ Pursuit of power _____

☐ _____

5. Read 2 Peter 3:10–14 and discuss the lasting value of the pursuits listed above. What is the consequence of a life spent in this way?

_____

_____

6. Read 1 Corinthians 3:10–15. If the fire described in this passage occurred today, what would be left of all you have done . . .

a. today? _____

b. this year? _____

c. in your life? _____

God grants every married couple the incredible privilege and responsibility of being used by Him to accomplish His work on planet earth. It is only as we know Him, yield to Him, and fulfill His purpose for us as a couple that we know the dignity which He designed for us as His children.

Construction
(to be completed as a couple)

1. Describe what you believe your marriage's mission *has been?*

_____

_____

_____

2. If needed, share any thoughts you might have of what this mission might be.

_____

_____

_____

3. Pray together and ask God to use the remainder of this session to help you focus on God's direction for your lives and marriage.

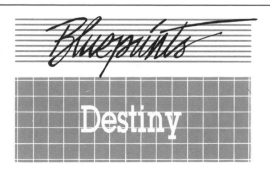

B. What Is Our Purpose?

> **HomeBuilders Principle #14:** A couple finds a sense of eternal value and self-esteem as they get to know God and invest their lives in the cause which will outlive them.

Psalm 119:105 says God's word is a "lamp to my feet and a light to my path," and it is from the Bible (along with the working of the Holy Spirit) that we determine what God expects from us as Christians. As we learn, yield, and submit our lives to God and His word we can be assured we are fulfilling God's purpose for our lives. When your mate is this confident in God's direction, you can see his sense of value and self-esteem grow.

1. Many of us are familiar with Ephesians 2:8–9 and how these verses assure us that we are saved by grace through faith in Christ. Yet we often fail to notice what Ephesians 2:10 says about God's purpose. Read this verse and discuss what it has to say about God's purpose for our lives.

_____

_____

2. What are God's "works" and purposes for you? Fill in the appropriate boxes on the next page after reading the texts.

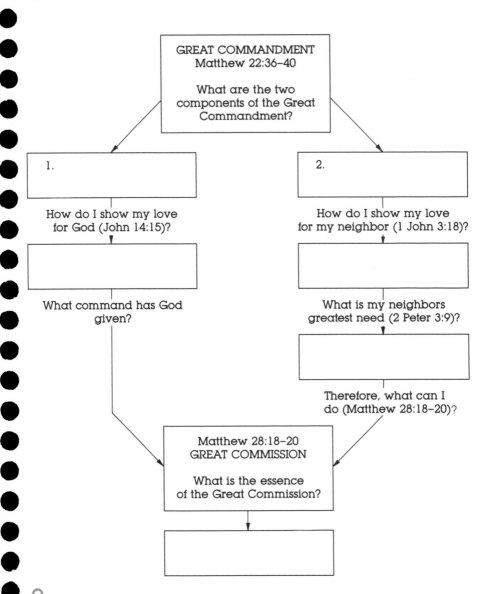

3. How do the Great Commandment and the Great Commission relate to your sense of direction as a couple?

_____

_____

(to be completed as a couple)

Describe what you believe your marriage's mission should be?

_____

_____

_____

Pray together and ask God to use the remainder of this session to help you continue to focus on God's direction for your lives and marriage.

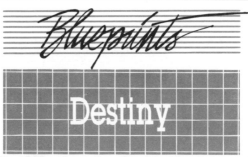

C. How Do We Apply God's Purpose in Our Marriage?

> Even if you're on the right track,
> you'll get run over
> if you just sit there.
> —Will Rogers

1. How have you as a couple been effective in fulfilling the Great Commandment? Share any practical ways you have expressed your love for God or for your neighbors.

_____

_____

2. As a couple, how have you been effective in fulfilling the Great Commission?

_____

_____

3. What are some practical ways you have helped someone become a disciple? How confident can you be that God really will accomplish His purposes ("good works") through your life and marriage? Discuss how these verses apply to your marriage:

a. Philippians 1:6

_____

_____

b. Philippians 2:13

_____

_____

c. Philippians 4:13

_____

_____

4. How can fulfilling God's purposes contribute to a healthy self-esteem?

_____

_____

5. How can a healthy self-esteem contribute to your ability to fulfill God's purposes?

_____

_____

> HomeBuilders Principle #15: Jesus Christ did not go to the
> cross just so we could have happy marriages or just a healthy
> self-esteem, but so that we would love Him, love one another,
> and go to the world with the greatest news ever announced.

6. Decide as a group whether to read your mission statements or to
focus on and encourage each couple by discussing how they could be
used for the kingdom of God. With either option, try to encourage each
couple with suggestions and affirmations of how they can apply their
gifts, talents, and abilities in the Great Commandment and the Great
Commission.

> And let us consider how we may
> spur one another on toward
> love and good deeds (Hebrews 10:24).

Record the observations others make of you in the space below.

_____

_____

_____

_____

> "By perseverance the snail
> reached the ark."
> C. H. Spurgeon

Make a date with your mate to meet in the next few days to complete **HomeBuilders Project #8**.

Date	Time	Location

■

Recommended Reading

Building Your Mate's Self-Esteem   by Dennis and Barbara Rainey

■ During the next four weeks you may want to read the following chapters and to complete the "Esteem Builder Projects" at the end of each chapter. This will help you and your mate establish a pattern of regular communication following this study, and will enrich you through the important concepts presented in these sections of the book which were not dealt with in the group. Set the dates now when you will complete each chapter and write them in the blanks below:

Chapter 8—Difficult Times   _____

Chapter 10—Pleasing Your Mate   _____

Chapter 11—Doing Right   _____

Chapter 12—Develop Friends   _____

As a Couple—5-10 Minutes

Review Session Eight and read the section entitled, "Where Do You Go from Here?" found at the end of this study.

Individually—20-25 Minutes

1. Do you ever hear yourself saying, "Somebody has got to do something about that issue" (or concern, or burden)? What current issues affect you in this way? Please list and explain.

_____

_____

_____

2. What "good works" could you offer that could have a positive impact on the issues you discussed in question 1?

a. Quickly write down any ideas you might have as to how you as a couple can be used in one or more of the following areas:

(1) Your local church _____

_____

(2) Prayer _____

_____

(3) Evangelism _____

_____

(4) Volunteering _____

_____

(5) Leading a **HomeBuilders** group or equipping marriages by bringing a group to the FamilyLife Marriage Conference in your area

_____

_____

(6) Giving—time, money, etc. _____

_____

(7) Joining a full-time ministry _____

_____

(8) Other _____

_____

b. Now select one thing that you as a couple can accomplish together for the kingdom of God. (Compare notes later.)

3. Review and refine the statement of what you wish you could do through your marriage to help fulfill the Great Commandment and the Great Commission. As a team, you and your mate can help make an impact on the world. In what areas, issues, and needs would you like to be involved?

_____

_____

_____

_____

4. Read over the following verses and observe what you learn about God's direction for your lives together.

Proverbs 16:9 _____

_____

Proverbs 3:5–6 _____

_____

Psalm 32:8 _____

_____

Psalm 37:3–5 _____

_____

Psalm 39:4–7 _____

_____

Interact As a Couple—25-30 Minutes

1. Compare your descriptions, then make one common description of vision and destiny for the growing impact of your marriage.

_____

_____

_____

_____

_____

_____

_____

2. Copy or type your statement and place it at work or home as a reminder of your mutual destiny. You may want to mount or frame it.

3. Write one major objective you wish to accomplish this year to help you achieve your mutual "divine destiny."

_____

_____

4. Send a copy of this completed project to your leader within 7-10 days.

5. Pray together now and in the weeks and months to come that God might grant you a mighty legacy.

ALTERNATIVE PROJECT
LEAVING A LEGACY THAT WILL OUTLIVE YOU

As a Couple—5–10 Minutes

Review the **CONSTRUCTION** project from Session Eight.

Read the section entitled, "Where Do You Go from Here?" found at the end of this study.

Individually—25–30 Minutes

1. If your life ended today, describe the legacy you would have left as an individual and as a couple.

_____

_____

2. What values are represented in the above statement?

_____

_____

3. a. Now imagine your life at age 70 (if you are 70, then add 15 years). What do you want it to be like? What do you envision you and your mate doing? Write out what you see. (Don't confine yourself to writing complete sentences. Jot down your thoughts, words, whatever comes to mind.)

_____

_____

_____

_____

b. Write out any steps you think you need to take today in order to get there. Put a star beside the steps you are presently taking.

(1) _____

_____

(2) _____

_____

(3) _____

_____

(4) _____

_____

(5) _____

_____

4. What values are represented in your answers to question #3?

_____

_____

5. Go back to the "mission statement" you wrote during Session Eight. Do you wish to make any changes? Record your new mission statement here.

_____

_____

6. Read Psalm 112:1-2 and apply it to your life, mate, and marriage. List one or two ways you can begin to leave this legacy.

a. _____

_____

b. _____

_____

Interact As a Couple—25–30 Minutes

1. Compare your descriptions, then make one common description of vision and destiny for the growing impact of your marriage.

_____

_____

_____

_____

_____

_____

_____

_____

2. Copy or type your statement and place it at work or home as a reminder of your mutual destiny. You may want to mount or frame it.

175

3. Write one major objective you wish to accomplish this year in helping you achieve your mutual "divine destiny."

_____

_____

_____

4. Send a copy of this completed project to your leader within seven to ten days.

5. Close your time in prayer that you might accomplish your objective.

Where do you go from here?

Where Do You Go from Here?

After eight sessions of focusing on building each other's self-esteem, it is our prayer that you and your mate have experienced a sense of renewed strength, confidence, and commitment to God and one another. Perhaps you have only noticed a few flickers of your victory torch. Or maybe your torch has burst into full flame during your times of interaction. In any case, you can be confident that you will continue to experience a steady deepening of your relationship with one another as each of you diligently seeks to build the other's sense of self-worth.

The key to this continued growth lies in your endurance in running the course of your life and marriage. Do not be disappointed when you do not experience an instant remedy for all the hurts you and your mate have experienced. Nor should you assume that you are "home free" because you have enjoyed some times of deep satisfaction together. Your marriage is God's provision to you and your mate for the long-distance run of life.

The central issue of this process is that you and your mate must look to Christ while attempting to build up one another. He will not disappoint you. He *does* answer prayer. He *is* at work in you and your mate. He *does* know what He is doing. Trust Him and keep growing strong in Him. Without Jesus Christ, no one can persevere in running the race. He is your hope!

Growing out of your partnership with Christ in your marriage will come a deepening of your commitment to His purpose to work through your marriage to touch the lives of others: your children, your friends, your neighbors, your church, your world. You can become part of a growing team of couples who are strengthening their own marriages and seeking to help others build godly homes as well. Just as you have grown by focusing on building up your mate, so will your marriage grow as the two of you focus on building up other couples.

Will you join with us in "Touching Lives . . . Changing Families"?

Here are nine practical ways you can continue to make a difference in your own family and also bring great benefit to many other families today:

1. If you are not a part of a growing church, join it and be baptized (if you haven't been baptized as a believer in Jesus Christ).

2. If you have not already done so, participate in *Building Your Marriage*, a life-changing study of God's blueprints for building intimacy in a marriage relationship. This first step in **The HomeBuilders Couples Series** has helped thousands of couples work together to strengthen their marriages.

3. Show the film, *Jesus*, on video as an evangelistic outreach in your neighborhood. For more information, write to:
> Inspirational Media
> 30012 Ivy Glenn Dr., Suite 200
> Laguna Niguel, CA 92677

4. If you have already completed **Building Your Marriage,** gather a group of couples (4-7) and lead them through a study of **Building Your Marriage, Building Your Mate's Self-Esteem,** or **Building Teamwork in Your Marriage.** And challenge other couples in your church or community to form new **HomeBuilders** groups.

5. Begin weekly family nights—having fun with your children and teaching them about Christ, the Bible, and the Christian life.

6. Host an Evangelistic Dinner Party—with another Christian couple, invite several non-Christian friends to your home and share your faith in Christ and the forgiveness of His gospel.

7. Share the good news of Jesus Christ with neighborhood children.

8. Invite one or more other couples to attend a FamilyLife Marriage Conference with you. (For a brochure of current cities and dates, write to the address listed below.)

9. If you have attended the FamilyLife Marriage Conference, talk with your pastor about helping to instruct premarrieds using the material you received.

Also, for information on any of the above ministry opportunities, a FamilyLife Marriage Conference brochure, or a free subscription to Dennis Rainey's monthly newsletter, "FamilyLife," write:

> FamilyLife
> P.O. Box 23840
> Little Rock, AR 72221-3840
> (501) 223-8663

About the Authors

Dennis and Barbara Rainey have long been partners in family-building—as marriage partners and parents, as staff members of Campus Crusade for Christ International, as FamilyLife Marriage Conference speakers, and as coauthors.

Dennis is Director of FamilyLife. A graduate of the University of Arkansas and Dallas Theological Seminary, he joined the staff of Campus Crusade for Christ International in 1970. He is general editor of this **HomeBuilders Couples Series** and is featured in **The HomeBuilders Film Series.** Barbara Rainey is also a graduate of the University of Arkansas, has been on the staff with Campus Crusade for 18 years, and has served as a FamilyLife Marriage Conference speaker for 12 years.

Together Dennis and Barbara Rainey have written *The Questions Book* and *Building Your Mate's Self-Esteem.* They are parents of six children—Ashley, Benjamin, Samuel, Rebecca, Deborah, and Laura—and they live in Little Rock, Arkansas.

The Four Spiritual Laws*

Just as there are physical laws that govern the physical universe, so are there spiritual laws which govern your relationship with God.

> **LAW ONE: God loves you and offers a wonderful plan for your life.**

God's Love

"For God so loved the world, that He gave His only begotten Son, that whoever believes in Him should not perish, but have eternal life" (John 3:16).

God's Plan

(Christ speaking) "I came that they might have life, and might have it abundantly" (that it might be full and meaningful) (John 10:10).

Why is it that most people are not experiencing the abundant life? Because . . .

> **LAW TWO: Man is sinful and separated from God. Therefore, he cannot know and experience God's love and plan for his life.**

Man Is Sinful

"For all have sinned and fall short of the glory of God" (Romans 3:23).

Man was created to have fellowship with God; but, because of his stubborn self-will, chose to go his own independent way, and

* Written by Bill Bright. Copyright © Campus Crusade for Christ, Inc., 1965, all rights reserved.

fellowship with God was broken. This self-will, characterized by an attitude of active rebellion or passive indifference, is evidence of what the Bible calls sin.

Man Is Separated

"For the wages of sin is death" (spiritual separation from God) (Romans 6:23).

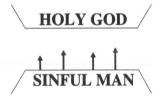

This diagram illustrates that God is holy and man is sinful. A great gulf separates the two. The arrows illustrate that man is continually trying to reach God and the abundant life through his own efforts, such as a good life, philosophy, or religion.

The third law explains the only way to bridge this gulf . . .

LAW THREE: Jesus Christ is God's only provision for man's sin. Through Him you can know and experience God's love and plan for your life.

He Died in Our Place

"But God demonstrates His own love toward us, in that while we were yet sinners, Christ died for us" (Romans 5:8).

He Rose from the Dead

"Christ died for our sins . . . He was buried . . . He was raised on the third day according to the Scriptures . . . He appeared to

[Peter], then to the twelve. After that He appeared to more than five hundred . . ." (1 Corinthians 15:3–6).

He Is the Only Way to God

"Jesus said to him, 'I am the way, and the truth, and the life; no one comes to the Father, but through Me'" (John 14:6).

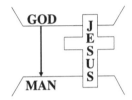

This diagram illustrates that God has bridged the gulf which separates us from Him by sending His Son, Jesus Christ, to die on the cross in our place to pay the penalty for our sins.

It is not enough just to know these three laws . . .

LAW FOUR: We must individually receive Jesus Christ as Savior and Lord; then we can know and experience God's love and plan for our lives.

We Must Receive Christ

"But as many as received Him, to them He gave the right to become children of God, even to those who believe in His name" (John 1:12).

We Receive Christ through Faith

"For by grace you have been saved through faith; and that not of yourselves, it is the gift of God; not as a result of works, that no one should boast" (Ephesians 2:8–9).

When We Receive Christ, We Experience a New Birth

(Read John 3:1–8.)

We Receive Christ by Personal Invitation

(Christ is speaking): "Behold, I stand at the door and knock; if any one hears My voice and opens the door, I will come in to him" (Revelation 3:20).

Receiving Christ involves turning to God from self (repentance) and trusting Christ to come into our lives to forgive our sins and to make us the kind of people He wants us to be. Just to agree intellectually that Jesus Christ is the Son of God and that He died on the cross for our sins is not enough. Nor is it enough to have an emotional experience. We receive Jesus Christ by faith, as an act of the will.

These two circles represent two kinds of lives:

SELF-DIRECTED LIFE

S —Self is on the throne
†—Christ is outside the life
• —Interests are directed by self, often resulting in discord and frustration

CHRIST-DIRECTED LIFE

†—Christ is in the life and on the throne
S —Self is yielding to Christ
• —Interests are directed by Christ, resulting in harmony with God's plan

Which circle best represents your life?
Which circle would you like to have represent your life?
The following explains how you can receive Christ:

You Can Receive Christ Right Now by Faith through Prayer

(Prayer is talking with God.)

God knows your heart and is not so concerned with your words as He is with the attitude of your heart. The following is a suggested prayer:

> *"Lord Jesus, I need You. Thank You for dying on the cross for my sins. I open the door of my life and receive You as my Savior and Lord. Thank You for forgiving my sins and giving me eternal life. Make me the kind of person You want me to be."*

Does this prayer express the desire of your heart?

If it does, pray this prayer right now, and Christ will come into your life, as He promised.

APPENDIX B

Have You Made the Wonderful Discovery of the Spirit-Filled Life?*

E very day can be an exciting adventure for the Christian who knows the reality of being filled with the Holy Spirit and who lives constantly, moment by moment, under His gracious control.

T he Bible tells us that there are three kinds of people:

1. NATURAL MAN (one who has not received Christ)

"But a natural man does not accept the things of the Spirit of God; for they are foolishness to him, and he cannot understand them, because they are spiritually appraised" (1 Corinthians 2:14).

SELF-DIRECTED LIFE

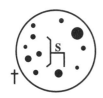

S—Ego or finite self is on the throne
†—Christ is outside the life
•—Interests are controlled by self, often resulting in discord and frustration

2. SPIRITUAL MAN (one who is controlled and empowered by the Holy Spirit)

"But he who is spiritual appraises all things . . ." (1 Corinthians 2:15).

CHRIST-DIRECTED LIFE

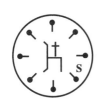

†—Christ is on the throne of the life
S—Ego or self is dethroned
•—Interests are under control of infinite God, resulting in harmony with God's plan

3. CARNAL MAN (one who has received Christ, but who lives in defeat because he trusts in his own efforts to live the Christian life)

SELF-DIRECTED LIFE

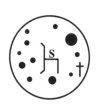

E—Ego or finite self is on the throne
†—Christ is dethroned
• —Interests are controlled by self, often resulting in discord and frustration

"And I, brethren, could not speak to you as to spiritual men, but as to carnal men, as to babes in Christ. I gave you milk to drink, not solid food; for you were not yet able to receive it. Indeed, even now you are not yet able, for you are still carnal. For since there is jealousy and strife among you, are you not fleshly, and are you not walking like mere men?" (1 Corinthians 3:1–3).

A. God has Provided for Us an Abundant and Fruitful Christian Life.

Jesus said, "I came that they might have life, and might have it abundantly" (John 10:10).

"I am the vine, you are the branches; he who abides in Me, and I in him, he bears much fruit; for apart from Me you can do nothing" (John 15:5).

"But the fruit of the Spirit is love, joy, peace, patience, kindness, goodness, faithfulness, gentleness, self-control; against such things there is no law" (Galatians 5:22, 23).

"But you shall receive power when the Holy Spirit has come upon you; and you shall be My witnesses both in Jerusalem, and in all Judea and Samaria, and even to the remotest part of the earth" (Acts 1:8).

THE SPIRITUAL MAN

Some Personal Traits Which Result from Trusting God:

Christ-centered
Empowered by the Holy Spirit
Introduces others to Christ
Effective prayer life
Understands God's Word
Trusts God
Obeys God

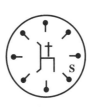

Love
Joy
Peace
Patience
Kindness
Goodness
Faithfulness

The degree to which these traits are manifested in the life depends upon the extent to which the Christian trusts the Lord with every detail of his life, and upon his maturity in Christ. One who is only beginning to understand the ministry of the Holy Spirit should not be discouraged if he is not as fruitful as more mature Christians who have known and experienced this truth for a longer period.

Why is it that most Christians are not experiencing the abundant life?

B. Carnal Christians Cannot Experience the Abundant and Fruitful Christian Life.

The carnal man trusts in his own efforts to live the Christian life:

1. He is either uninformed about, or has forgotten, God's love, forgiveness, and power (Romans 5:8–10; Hebrews 10:1–25; 1 John 1; 2:1–3; 2 Peter 1:9; Acts 1:8).

2. He has an up-and-down spiritual experience.

3. He cannot understand himself—he wants to do what is right, but cannot.

4. He fails to draw upon the power of the Holy Spirit to live the Christian life.

(1 Corinthians 3:1–3; Romans 7:15–24; 8:7; Galatians 5:16–18)

THE CARNAL MAN

Some or all of the following traits may characterize the Christian who does not fully trust God:

Ignorance of his
   spiritual heritage
Unbelief
Disobedience
Loss of love for God and
   for others
Poor prayer life
No desire for Bible study

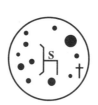

Legalistic attitude
Discouragement
Impure thoughts
Jealousy
Guilt
Critical spirit
Worry
Frustration
Aimlessness

(The individual who professes to be a Christian but who continues to practice sin should realize that he may not be a Christian at all, according to 1 John 2:3; 3:6–9; Ephesians 5:5.)

The third truth gives us the only solution to this problem . . .

C. Jesus Promised the Abundant and Fruitful Life as the Result of Being Filled (Controlled and Empowered) by the Holy Spirit.

The Spirit-filled life is the Christ-controlled life, by which Christ lives His life in and through us in the power of the Holy Spirit (John 15).

1. One becomes a Christian through the ministry of the Holy Spirit, according to John 3:1–8. From the moment of spiritual birth, the Christian is indwelt by the Holy Spirit at all times (John 1:12; Colossians 2:9–10; John 14:16–17). Though all Christians are indwelt by the Holy Spirit, not all Christians are filled (controlled and empowered) by the Holy Spirit.

2. The Holy Spirit is the source of the overflowing life (John 7:37–39).

3. The Holy Spirit came to glorify Christ (John 16:1–5). When one is filled with the Holy Spirit, he is a true disciple of Christ.

4. In His last command before His ascension, Christ promised the power of the Holy Spirit to enable us to be witnesses for Him (Acts 1:1–9).

How, then, can one be filled with the Holy Spirit?

D. We Are Filled (Controlled and Empowered) by the Holy Spirit by Faith; Then We Can Experience the Abundant and Fruitful Life Which Christ Promised to Each Christian.

You can appropriate the filling of the Holy Spirit *right now* if you:

1. Sincerely desire to be controlled and empowered by the Holy Spirit (Matthew 5:6; John 7:37–39).

2. Confess your sins.

By faith thank God that He has forgiven all of your sins—past, present, and future—because Christ died for you (Colossians 2:13–15; 1 John 1; 2:1–3; Hebrews 10:1–17).

3. By faith claim the fullness of the Holy Spirit, according to:

a. HIS COMMAND—Be filled with the Spirit. "And do not get drunk with wine, for that is dissipation, but be filled with the Spirit" (Ephesians 5:18).

b. HIS PROMISE—He will always answer when we pray according to His will. "And this is the confidence which we have before Him, that, if we ask anything according to His will, He hears us. And if we know that He hears us in whatever we ask, we know that we have the requests which we have asked from Him" (1 John 5:14–15).

Faith can be expressed through prayer . . .

193

How to Pray in Faith to Be Filled with the Holy Spirit

We are filled with the Holy Spirit by *faith* alone. However, true prayer is one way of expressing your faith. The following is a suggested prayer:

> "*Dear Father, I need You. I acknowledge that I have been in control of my life; and that, as a result, I have sinned against You. I thank You that You have forgiven my sins through Christ's death on the cross for me. I now invite Christ to again take control of the throne of my life. Fill me with the Holy Spirit as You commanded me to be filled, and as You promised in your Word that You would do if I asked in faith. I pray this in the name of Jesus. As an expression of my faith, I now thank You for taking control of my life and for filling me with the Holy Spirit.*"

Does this prayer express the desire of your heart? If so, bow in prayer and trust God to fill you with the Holy Spirit right now.

How to Know that You are Filled (Controlled and Empowered) by the Holy Spirit

Did you ask God to fill you with the Holy Spirit? Do you know that you are now filled with the Holy Spirit? On what authority? (On the trustworthiness of God Himself and His Word: Hebrews 11:6; Romans 14:22–23).

Do not depend upon feelings. The promise of God's Word, not our feelings, is our authority. The Christian lives by faith (trust) in the trustworthiness of God Himself and His Word. This train diagram illustrates the relationship between **fact** (God and His Word), **faith** (our trust in God and His Word), and **feeling** (the result of our faith and obedience) (John 14:21).

The train will run with or without the caboose. However, it would be futile to attempt to pull the train by the caboose. In the same way, we, as Christians, do not depend upon feelings or emotions, but we place our faith (trust) in the trustworthiness of God and the promises of His Word.

How to Walk in the Spirit

Faith (trust in God and His promises) is the only means by which a Christian can live the Spirit-controlled life. As you continue to trust Christ moment by moment:

1. Your life will demonstrate more and more of the fruit of the Spirit (Galatians 5:22–23); and will be more and more conformed to the image of Christ (Romans 12:2; 2 Corinthians 3:18).

2. Your prayer life and study of God's Word will become more meaningful.

3. You will experience His power in witnessing (Acts 1:8).

4. You will be prepared for spiritual conflict against the world (1 John 2:15–17); against the flesh (Galatians 5:16–17); and against Satan (1 Peter 5:7–9; Ephesians 6:10–13).

5. You will experience His power to resist temptation and sin (1 Corinthians 10:13; Philippians 4:13; Ephesians 1:19–23; 6:10; 2 Timothy 1:7; Romans 6;1–16).

Spiritual Breathing

By faith you can continue to experience God's love and forgiveness.

If you become aware of an area of your life (an attitude or an action) that is displeasing to the Lord, even though you are walking with Him and sincerely desiring to serve Him, simply thank God that

He has forgiven your sins—past, present and future—on the basis of Christ's death on the cross. Claim His love and forgiveness by faith and continue to have fellowship with Him.

If you retake the throne of your life through sin—a definite act of disobedience—breathe spiritually.

Spiritual Breathing (exhaling the impure and inhaling the pure) is an exercise in faith that enables you to continue to experience God's love and forgiveness.

1. EXHALE—confess your sin—agree with God concerning your sin and thank Him for His forgiveness of it, according to 1 John 1:9 and Hebrews 10:1–25. Confession involves repentance—a change in attitude and action.

2. INHALE—surrender the control of your life to Christ, and appropriate (receive) the fullness of the Holy Spirit by faith. Trust that He now controls and empowers you, according to the *command* of Ephesians 5:18 and the *promise* of 1 John 5:14–15.

Renew Your Commitment.

You've been working on the most important commitment of your life—spending time with God and with your spouse. No doubt you've learned a lot of things about your mate that will help the two of you grow closer together for years to come. You've also learned a lot about God's Word and how much it means to study the Bible with each other. But don't let it stop here—lay the next block in the foundation of your marriage by beginning the HomeBuilders Couples Series®. It will help you keep your marriage as strong, as dynamic, as solid as the day you said "I do."

Building Your Marriage
By Dennis Rainey
Help couples get closer together than you ever imagined possible.
•Leader's Guide
ISBN 08307.16130
•Study Guide
ISBN 08307.16122

Building Your Mate's Self-Esteem
By Dennis & Barbara Rainey
Marriage is God's workshop for self-esteem.
•Leader's Guide
ISBN 08307.16173
•Study Guide
ISBN 08307.16165

Building Teamwork in Your Marriage
By Robert Lewis
Help couples celebrate and enjoy their differences
•Leader's Guide
ISBN 08307.16157
•Study Guide
ISBN 08307.16149

Resolving Conflict in Your Marriage
By Bob & Jan Horner
Turn conflict into love and understanding.
•Leader's Guide
ISBN 08307.16203
•Study Guide
ISBN 08307.16181

Mastering Money in Your Marriage
By Ron Blue
Put an end to conflicts and find out how to use money to glorify God.
•Leader's Guide
ISBN 08307.16254
•Study Guide
ISBN 08307.16246

Growing Together In Christ
By David Sunde
Discover how Christ is central to your marriage.
•Leader's Guide
ISBN 08307.16297
•Study Guide
ISBN 08307.16289

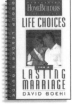

Life Choices for a Lasting Marriage
By David Boehi
Find out how to make the right choices in your marriage.
•Leader's Guide
ISBN 08307.16262
•Study Guide
ISBN 08307.16270

Managing Pressure in Your Marriage
By Dennis Rainey & Robert Lewis
Learn how obedience to God will take pressure off your marriage
•Leader's Guide
ISBN 08307.16319
•Study Guide
ISBN 08307.16300

Expressing Love in Your Marriage
By Jerry & Sheryl Wunder and Dennis & Jill Eenigenburg
Discover God's plan for your love life by seeking God's best for your mate.
•Leader's Guide
ISBN 08307.16661
•Study Guide
ISBN 08307.16688

"A Weekend to Remember"

Every couple has a unique set of needs. The FamilyLife Marriage Conference meets couples' needs by equipping them with proven solutions that address practically every component of "How to Build a Better Marriage." The conference gives you the opportunity to slow down and focus on your spouse and your relationship. You will spend an insightful weekend together, doing fun couples' projects and hearing from dynamic speakers on real-life solutions for building and enhancing oneness in your marriage.

You'll learn:

- *Five secrets of successful marriage*
- *How to implement oneness in your marriage*
- *How to maintain a vital sexual relationship*
- *How to handle conflict*
- *How to express forgiveness to one another*

Our insightful speaker teams also conduct sessions for:

- *Soon-to-be-marrieds*
- *Men-only*
- *Women-only*

The FamilyLife Marriage Conference

To register or receive a free brochure and schedule, call
FamilyLife at 1-800-333-1433.

FAMILYLIFE

A ministry of Campus Crusade for Christ International

Take a Weekend...to Raise Your Children for a Lifetime

Good parents aren't just born that way; they begin with a strong, biblical foundation and then work at improving their parenting skills. That's where we come in.

In one weekend the FamilyLife Parenting Conference will equip you with the principles and tools you need to be more effective parents for a lifetime. Whether you're just getting started or in the turbulent years of adolescence, we'll show you the biblical blueprints for raising your children. You'll hear from dynamic speakers and do fun parenting skills projects designed to help you apply what you've learned. You'll receive proven, effective principles from parents just like you who have dedicated their lives to helping families.

You'll learn how to:

◆ *Build a strong relationship with your child*

◆ *Help your child develop emotional, spiritual and sexual identity*

◆ *Develop moral character in your child*

◆ *Give your child a sense of mission*

◆ *Pass on your values to your child*

The FamilyLife Parenting Conference
To register or receive a free brochure and schedule, call
FamilyLife at 1-800-333-1433.

FamilyLife
A ministry of Campus Crusade for Christ International

FamilyLife Resources

Building Your Mate's Self-Esteem

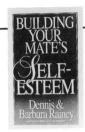

The key to a joy-filled marriage is a strong sense of self-worth in both partners. This practical, best-selling book helps you tap into God's formula for building up your mate. How to overcome problems from the past, how to help your mate conquer self-doubt, how to boost communication, and much more. Creative "Esteem-Builder Projects" will bring immediate results, making your marriage all it can be. The #1 best-seller at FamilyLife Marriage Conferences across America. **Paperback, $8.95**

Pulling Weeds, Planting Seeds

Thirty-eight insightful, thought-provoking chapters, laced with humor, show how you can apply the wisdom of God's Word to your life and home. Includes chapters on making your time with your family count, dealing with tough situations at home and at work, living a life of no regrets, and MUCH MORE. These bite-sized, fun-to-read chapters make this great book hard to put down. **Hardcover, $12.95**

Staying Close

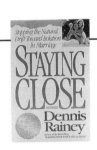

Overcome the isolation that creeps into so many marriages, and watch your marriage blossom! This best-selling book, winner of the 1990 Gold Medallion Award for best book on marriage and family, is packed with practical ideas and HomeBuilders projects to help you experience the oneness God designed for your marriage. How to manage stress. How to handle conflict. How to be a great lover. And much more! Based on 15 years of research and favorite content from the FamilyLife Marriage Conference. **Paperback, $10.95**

The Questions Book

Discover the miracle of truly understanding each other. This book will lead you into deeper intimacy and joy by giving you 31 sets of fun, thought-provoking questions you can explore and answer together. Space is provided for you to write your answers. Share your innermost feelings, thoughts, goals, and dreams. This book could lead to the best times you'll ever spend together. **Hardcover, $9.95**

For more information on these and other FamilyLife Resources contact your local Christian retailer or call FamilyLife at 1-800-333-1433.

The HomeBuilders

C O U P L E S   S E R I E S

"Unless the Lord builds the house,
they labor in vain who build it."
Psalm 127:1

HomeBuilders Evaluation

Your First Name _____ Last Name _____

Spouse's First Name _____ Wedding Date _____ Your Age _____

Home Phone _____ Work Phone _____

Address _____

City _____ State _____ ZIP Code _____

Full Church Name _____

Church City _____ State _____

May we quote you?
❑ Yes   ❑ No

How would you rate this HomeBuilders Couples study?

	Poor							Excellent		
Overall experience	1	2	3	4	5	6	7	8	9	10
Study Guide	1	2	3	4	5	6	7	8	9	10

How many HomeBuilders Couples Series have you now participated in ? [   ]
Describe the effect this HomeBuilders study has had on you and your family:

How would you change or improve this HomeBuilders study?

Would you be willing to lead a separate HomeBuilders study yourself?
❑ Yes   ❑ No   ❑ Yes, with more training

Have you attended a FamilyLife Conference? ❑ Yes ❑ No

FamilyLife has many other resources for you and your family. Please check if you would like to receive additional information on the following resources:
❑ Other HomeBuilders Couples Series studies
❑ FamilyLife Marriage Conference
❑ FamilyLife Parenting Conference
❑ "FamilyLife Today" radio program
❑ Books, videos and tapes

BUSINESS REPLY MAIL

FIRST-CLASS MAIL   PERMIT NO. 4092   LITTLE ROCK, AR

POSTAGE WILL BE PAID BY ADDRESSEE

FAMILY LIFE
P O BOX 23840
LITTLE ROCK AR 72221-9940